I0116549

The Instant Celebrity

The Instant Celebrity

The Instant Celebrity

Their 15 Minutes of Fame, Notoriety or Whatever

by

Tanya Slover

The Instant Celebrity

The Instant Celebrity:
Their 15 Minutes of Fame, Notoriety or Whatever

First Edition 2012
Published by Invisibird Books

Copyright © 2012 by Tanya Slover

Interior images © www.arttoday.com
www.clipart.com
www.openclipart.org

Cover Design by Tanya Slover

ISBN-13: 978-0615649504
ISBN-10: 0615649505

FOREWORD

In 1968 pop artist, Andy Warhol, got it right when he said "In the future, everybody will be famous for 15 minutes." The tabloids, the internet, social media, reality television and the 24/7 news cycle has spawned a culture of fame unlike even Warhol might have imagined. People can now become famous, more often than not, for absolutely nothing - certainly not talent or hard work.

In pursuit of their 15 minutes the famous wannabes will do almost anything - the unimaginable, the obnoxious, the outrageous and shameless, the shocking and desperate, demeaning themselves on reality TV and, in some cases, committing unthinkable crimes. Such is their narcissistic need for recognition and the coveted brass ring of Instant Celebrity.

Some people, however, come by fame accidentally, such as Captain Chesley "Sulley" Sullenberger who safely piloted the US Airways jet into the Hudson in 2009 and saved the lives of everyone on board. Such unintended celebrities are rare and their unsought fame thankfully not so short-lived. Still other people rise out of obscurity as a result of some nefarious or criminal activity. Pop culture, in fact, seems to have an abiding interest in the notorious, corrupt and murderous ones among us. Ever at the ready, the media obliges this morbid curiosity.

As we all know, the fame game doesn't require talent or intellect, moral rectitude, brains, good looks or personality, and it makes a lot of people very rich. For a glimpse of how Pygmalion in reverse works just tune into an episode of *Jersey Shore*. While its cast of characters may ooze an odd, even beastly, fascination for some viewers there are still those out there who would rather dance with a grizzly bear than be subjected to such mind-numbing vacuity.

The seismic shift in our culture was recently noted in a UCLA study of tween girls who were asked to rate their values. Fame jumped from 15th in 1997 to 1st place in 2011. Hands down the tweeners' desire for fame trumped things like financial success, physical fitness, sense of community and benevolence. One of the co-authors of the study, Patricia Greenfield, noted, "The rise of fame in preteen television may be one influence in the documented rise of narcissism in our culture."

Celebrity wannabes believe that just because they live, breathe, and take up space they are entitled to it all. Their narcissism tells them they are special creatures worthy of fame and fortune, merited or not. As inane and perverse as this might seem, it is the new normal and today's dizzying array of reality shows (a flavor and stripe for every taste) are presently one of the best ways wannabes can feed their narcissism and go after their 15 minutes. Once in a while, however, a real talent does show up and fortunately for us, their celebrity endures.

The Instant Celebrity

Who said, "In the future everybody will be famous for fifteen minutes"?

Andy Warhol, the 60s pop artist with the moppish shock of white-blond hair. His gritty docudrama style, film shorts, and iconic renderings of Marilyn Monroe, Coca Cola and Campbell soup cans made him internationally famous. Long before reality television came along he got it right when he said there would be a time when people would become famous for absolutely nothing at all.

What star of the popular television series, *Madmen*, summed up the Instant Celebrity phenomenon as well as anyone?

Jon Hamm. The actor minced no words when he told the April, 2012, issue of *Elle UK*, "Whether it's Kim Kardashian or Paris Hilton or whoever, stupidity is certainly celebrated. Being a f***ing idiot is a valuable commodity in this culture because you're rewarded significantly."

Needless to say, Kim was not happy with Jon's stinging observation and tweeted, "Calling someone who runs their own business, is part of a successful TV show, produces, writes, designs, and creates, 'stupid,' is in my opinion careless." She said everyone in the business worked hard and they all had to respect each other.

If Kardashian thought Hamm might soften and/or retract his words, she was wrong. In an interview with Matt Lauer on the *Today Show* the actor later defended his words to *Elle* magazine. "I don't think they were careless; I think they were accurate." Ouch!

What media-savvy Instant Celebrity emerged from a 22-day stint in jail in 2007 and humbly uttered, "I am not the same person I was. God has given me this new chance"?

Paris Hilton – just as humbly, one might add, as Hollywood pie. Some will no doubt remember, but have mercifully forgotten, that Ms. Hilton's 15-minute star was launched into the stratosphere several years earlier when a video showing her having sex went viral on the internet. Dubbed *One Night in Paris*, the raunchy romp with beau, Rick Salomon, left nothing to the imagination and created a whole new legion of pervy fans. Media rags went into a feeding frenzy and paid top dollar for every bit of additional trash anyone could come up with about the life and times of Ms. Hilton.

Paris's 2001 pornographic video was supposedly never intended for public consumption. Rick Salomon is said to have released it for profit just before the debut of Paris Hilton and Nicole Ritchie's television reality show, *The Simple Life*, in June of 2003.

The release of the video tape spawned suits and countersuits between the two horny protagonists and an explanation from Ms. Hilton that she was "out of it" at the time of the video's filming. Whatever the case, the sex tape was an instant worldwide success depicting what many considered at the time to be the most graphic celebrity sex yet seen on the internet.

How can those who have already achieved some degree of celebrity sometimes turn their addictions into a bid for more celebrity?

By getting on *Celebrity Rehab*, yet another reality show, and dealing with their problem in front of millions of viewers. Using this forum to rehabilitate themselves may also help rehabilitate their flagging, if not already, ex-careers. It doesn't always work but at least the show does. It's currently in its fifth season.

Whose debatable talent for birthing multiple babies turned one woman into an Instant Celebrity and a media punching bag?

Nadya Suleman aka the Octomom. The mother of four daughters and ten sons, Nayda rose to instant international attention in 2009 when she gave birth to live octuplets who have since survived and thrived - a rare event in large multiple births.

Suleman was vilified by the press when it was discovered that she had six other children in addition to the octuplets and was reportedly on public assistance. A claim she originally denied. The press was also unhappy with the fact she was unemployed. How you might raise 14 kids and also have a job was never made clear by her critics.

Since bursting onto the Instant Celebrity scene the Octomom has tested the waters of several possible careers in hopes of one day becoming the sole financial support for her brood. Among other endeavors, Nayda just finished an adult entertainment film called *Octomom Home Alone* starring no one but her in which she pleasures herself. She claims to have been celibate for over 13 years and had never even touched herself before doing the video.

An artful liar and/or perhaps just an artful self-promoter, Suleman apparently knows the value of provocative PR. She is also said to be checking into doing some strip tease for profit as well as endorsing a coupon company. Additionally, she endorsed a quickie loan outfit for people in dire straits called Octoloan.

Why all the frenetic entrepreneurial activity? The Octomom claims she wants no help from the state and will do whatever it takes to be independent as possible. Whatever - one thing is for sure, the Octomom will keep on extending her 15 minutes for as long as she can come up with new ways to grab the spotlight and so far, she has managed to do just that.

What homeless man with "the golden voice" was rediscovered on a Columbus, Ohio street corner in 2010?

Ted Williams. After a clip went viral on the internet showing him and hearing his self-proclaimed "God-given gift of a great voice," the media and others instantly courted the former radio announcer and bestowed endless perks on him including guest appearances on network TV shows, a commercial selling Kraft Macaroni and Cheese, a place to live and several stints in rehab. Before "the golden voice" ended up on the streets because of drugs, he had been a very successful radio personality and a voice-over artist. Given a second chance at celebrity, Ted is anxious to get back to work and prove why he's worth another 15 minutes.

What aspiring starlet became famous only after her death, known posthumously as "The Black Dahlia"?

Elizabeth Short. Her horribly mutilated body was discovered in a vacant lot near the Baldwin Hills area of Los Angeles. It had been severed in half and grotesquely posed. Elizabeth Short's murder has never been solved and was the grisly inspiration for several Hollywood films including *The Black Dahlia* in 2006 and *True Confessions* released back in 1981.

Why Elizabeth Short was called The Black Dahlia is the subject of speculation. Some sources claim the name of a film released just before her death called *The Blue Dahlia*, along with the black clothes she often wore and her dyed black hair, inspired the nickname. Others say it has a much simpler explanation – the dahlia the starlet sometimes wore in her hair. Whatever the reason for the moniker, one thing is for sure - it was Elizabeth Short's shocking murder that made her famous.

What teenager gained instant notoriety after shooting her 36-year old lover's wife in the face?

Amy Fisher. The 16-year old shot Joey Buttafuoco's wife in 1991 after he refused to get a divorce. "The Long Island Lolita," as the press dubbed Amy, was convicted and sent to prison for seven years. The nubile sex pot's brush with fame resulted, not surprisingly, in two TV movies, one of them starring Drew Barrymore.

Note: Mrs. Buttafuoco survived the shooting but ended up deaf in one ear and with one side of her face partially paralyzed. She dumped her husband, Joey, who served six months for statutory rape and has remained the enduring butt of many Buttafuoco-cradle-robbing jokes ever since.

What was the name of Michael Jackson's doctor at the time of the singer's death?

If you can't recall, you're probably not alone. In spite of the extensive media coverage of Jackson's trial most people have already forgotten Dr. Conrad Murray's name.

What unusual commodity did Natalie Dylan auction off over the internet that made her famous for more than a few news cycles?

Her virginity. The odd offering made the 22-year old woman famous, notorious, whatever. The highest bidder offered her 3.8 million for first time privileges in 2009 then backed out. Natalie reportedly kept his hefty deposit and went on to ink a book deal. Would you have expected less? These days book companies invariably line up to publish sensational claptrap if they think it will turn a dime and, in so doing, turn nobodies into the briefest of celebrities.

Why was Brian Jerard Kaelin, aka Kato, suddenly launched into the Instant Celebrity stratosphere for 15 minutes?

He was a witness at the O.J. Simpson trial, the so-called trial of the century in the mid-nineties. Kato was staying in the guest house located on O.J.'s property the night Nicole Brown Simpson and Ronald Goldman were brutally murdered and reportedly observed the celebrity's movements before and after the double homicide.

During the trial Kato contradicted the ex-NFL star's defense was on several key points but, because much of his testimony so was incoherent and rambling, he failed to help the state with their case against Simpson. Many who attended the trial and/or saw it on television felt Kato – looking every bit the persona of California's laid back surfer-type - was hiding something, was afraid, or was just plain dumb.

Before basking in the Instant Celebrity limelight, Kato Kaelin acted in several low-budget movies. Unable to successfully capitalize on his 15 minutes after the famous trial, he slipped back into obscurity and then resurfaced some years later to host a radio show, "Tailgating with Kato." To this day Kato claims he did not seek celebrity, it simple found him when he testified at O.J.'s trial.

In a September, 2012 appearance on *The Dr. Drew Show*, Kato once again denied having any first-hand information as to whether O.J. had murdered his wife or not, but said he thought the ex-NFL running back might be guilty. He ended the show by saying, "Be a moth, choose the light." Just what does that mean? No wonder he confounded prosecutor, Marcia Clark, during the trial and, as a result, she declared him a hostile witness.

Note: Though O.J. Simpson was never convicted of the gruesome murders of his ex-wife and Ronald

Goldman, he did however finally go to jail on unrelated charges. In 2008 he was found guilty of kidnapping and armed robbery stemming from an attempt to recover memorabilia from his football career which he claimed had been stolen from him. Just goes to show how fickle fame is and how fast it can turn into infamy. Number 32 will now most likely be remembered more for his notorious deeds than for the yardage he piled up as a running back.

What Hollywood madam gained instant international notoriety when her prostitution ring was busted in the mid-nineties?

Heidi Fleiss, the famous Madam to Hollywood stars, billionaires, politicos and the corporate elite. Of her work she humbly commented, "I took the oldest profession on earth and I did it better than anyone on earth. Alexander the Great conquered the world at 32. I conquered it at 22."

Convicted in 1997 on tax evasion and money laundering, Heidi was imprisoned for 23 months. After her release, she tried unsuccessfully to start her own brothel in Nevada. She later put out a line of clothing known as Heidi Wear Clothing.

How have some morbidly obese people turned their liability into a potential asset for achieving Instant Celebrity?

By competing to lose weight with other corpulent souls on the television reality show, *The Biggest Loser*. Whoever shreds the most poundage, wins and enjoys a slimmer, healthier body, for however long, and the fleeting admiration of their viewer fans.

Why was Warren Jeffs ignominiously dubbed the "Perv Prophet" while in jail awaiting his trial on statutory rape?

The leader of the Fundamentalist Church of Jesus Christ of Latter Day Saints, a radical offshoot of Mormonism, was apparently suffering from sexual withdrawal and resorted to compulsive masturbation – up to as many as 15 times a day according to one of his former jailers. If true, then it is a bit hypocritical of the self-proclaimed messiah since he told the men in his church that masturbation offended God. All bets were off once Jeffs himself no longer had access to all the sex he wanted with his many wives and underaged girls. What offended the Lord then was suddenly moot.

Jeffs' ungodly fifteen minutes has rapidly gone by the wayside along with the key that he preached turned the gates to heaven – polygamy - a core belief he will not be able to practice for a long time, at least not with the girls.

What old cowboy's unique ranch has turned him into an Instant Celebrity of sorts?

Stanley Marsh III's Cadillac Ranch outside Amarillo, Texas, draws countless visitors every year. It's not the typical ranch you might envision but rather one of up-ended Cadillacs buried nose down in the dirt. This public art exhibition has made Stanley March III an Instant Celebrity and is a magnet for thousands of people driving along storied Route 66. Fans visit this installation in droves and paint and scribble their grafitti all over the Cadillacs. Marsh doesn't mind. He encourages it.

Whose 15 minutes of fame in a 2000 TV reality show led to a nude gig in *Playboy Magazine* and a boxing match with an Olympic gymnastic champion?

Darva Conger, an emergency room nurse. She was named the winner of the television reality show, *Who Wants to Marry a Multi-Millionaire*," after being picked by the show's bachelor, Rick Rockwell, to be his bride. After an ever so brief honeymoon, Darva had the marriage annulled and went on to pose nude in *Playboy* that same year.

Some years later Ms. Conger sparred off with Olympic gymnastics champion, Olga Corbut, in the boxing ring and actually won the decision. Apparently some media divas will do just about anything for another 15 minutes. From the ER to reality TV to *Playboy* to boxing, what's next or did Darva's 15 minutes of fame finally flame out?

What was Patricia Krentcil's brief claim to the fame spotlight in 2012?

Her deep, leathery mahogany tan – so much so that "tanning mom," Patricia Krentcil, became the caricature of a suntan and was spoofed because of it on *Saturday Night Live*. Seth Meyers said the woman's tanning bed obsession had toasted her until she "looked like a baseball glove." Kristen Wiig joined in the skit on *SNL* and placed two pieces of bread between her knees until they started smoking. Then voilá, she produced two pieces of burned toast.

Patricia Krentcil's flash in the celebrity pan all started because she allegedly took her five-year old daughter tanning with her and was charged with child endangerment. Whether or not her little peanut got roasted as well is not clear.

Apparently, in the days before Krentcil became a tanorexic*, she was sexy and attractive. Modeling pictures, admittedly some years old, show what a looker she was back in the day.

* Yes, there is really a word for the tanning mom's obsession. It is called *tanorexia* which is an addiction, whether psychological or physical, to sunbathing and/or tanning beds.

There are studies suggesting that there is a release of endorphins in some people while tanning and, if they stop, they suffer withdrawal symptoms. *Tanorexia* is now squarely in the spotlight thanks to Patricia Krenctil.

Whose celebrity came quite by accident when a picture of him as a geeky teenager with a mouthful of braces went viral on the internet?

"Bad Luck Brian" whose real name is supposedly not Brian at all, but is said to be Dick Butts. Whatever the real name, the nerdy picture of "Brian" became the butt of one too many jokes associated with off-putting or embarrassing situations, being a loser and/or someone who just cannot catch a break. As a result, "Bad Luck Brian" is now a popular meme*.

 * An idea or behavior, symbol, etc., that rapidly replicates, spreading from one person to another, and changing in response to cultural pressures.

What All-American, fresh-faced girl was pictured with a baby on the Ivory Snow laundry box in the early '70s before becoming a porn star?

Pure-as-a-drift-of-snow Marilyn Chambers. However, it was her talent behind *The Green Door*, the 1972 classic porn film, that ended up bringing her greater though more dubious fame.

What "dead thing" shuffled through its 15 minutes and became such a terrifying media presence in 2012 the CDC had to release a statement allaying public fears about it?

The zombie. Apparently, a rash of internet rumors about widespread cannibalism triggered a CNN media release by the CDC on June 4, 2012, denying the existence of zombies stating, "It does not know of a virus that would reanimate the dead." You really know the "braineaters" are enjoying their notoriety when the CDC officially has to refute them and has the internet afire with rumors about the awful things "the walking dead" do to the living.

The "zombie apocalypse" has been fueled not only by a popular TV show about them but also by a spate of bizarre news stories including one about a man in Miami, Florida, who chewed off 75% of a homeless man's face. The man's mother had to vehemently defend her son saying the media's characterization of him had been unfair stating unequivocally her son was "not a zombie."

Even Mila Kunis of *The Black Swan* got into the media zombie brouhaha in June, 2012, when she fearfully announced her now jailed stalker might "try and eat her" if he got a chance.

Popular culture has embraced "the braineaters" and

they currently seem to be having much more staying power in the media than the living things looking for their 15 minutes.

Note: In zombie folklore "braineaters" are so dubbed because the brains and blood they consume reanimate and strengthen the walking dead.

What six-year old boy became an Instant Celebrity for a widely reported balloon trip he never took?

Falcon Heene, or the Balloon Boy as he is now known. Falcon's father frantically called 911 reporting that his young son had climbed into a helium-filled balloon and was accidentally lofted 8,000 feet into the skies.

The news channels and its viewers anxiously followed the errant balloon until it crashed landed some hours later. Everyone expected the worst, thinking young

Falcon had fallen to his death, only to discover the boy had never been in the balloon at all but was hiding safely in his attic back at home.

When Falcon Heene was interviewed along with his family on *Larry King* a short time later and the boy was asked why he didn't respond to his father's calls at home to come out of the attic, Balloon Boy fidgeted in his chair and said, "You guys said that, um, we did this for the show."

The Balloon Boy inadvertently exposed his family's inventive scheme to try and get enough media attention focused on them so the Heenes might parlay it into their own reality show. It didn't work.

How did the notorious serial killer, Jeffery Damher, dispose of his victims?

He harvested and refrigerated many of their organs and cannibalized them at his leisure. He said that he suffered from loneliness and that by eating his victims they became a part of him forever. As sick as this sounds, Damher's unthinkable crimes made him famous, notorious/whatever, for a brief moment.

Dahmer was convicted and sentenced to life in prison where he was bludgeoned to death in 1994 by a fellow inmate.

Whose narcissistic need for fame and attention ended in the sadistic killing of his roommate in 2012 with an uploaded video showing it on the internet?

Luka Magnotta. A porn actor and high-end escort, the latter characterization according to him, murdered and dismembered his roommate and lover then ate part of his flesh. He also performed sex acts on the corpse for viewers to see on the worldwide web.

When he was finished with the body, he sent parts of it to the police and various politicians. Magnotta then fled from Canada to France and on to Berlin, Germany, where he was arrested in an internet café while watching himself on the news.

In an interview Magnotta gave before becoming a killer he told the viewing audience, "Everybody likes me." What narcissistic fame-seeker does not believe that? If what he thought was true about himself before he committed his horrific crime, what does he think now after all the attention?

Before Mangotta's video clip of the murder and dismemberment was taken off the internet, it had over

300,000 hits and quite a few words of sick admiration from those as pathologically gone as he was.

What female intern dreamily remarked after trysting with the President of the United States in the Oval Office that they were "sexual soul mates?"

Monica Lewinsky of blue dress fame. The "sexual soul mate" to which she referred was Bill Clinton. For those who too young to remember, or who were off in some alternate universe at the time of President Clinton's impeachment hearings, Lewinsky's blue dress was the dress she refused to have dry cleaned after cavorting with the president.

Whether the dress was kept as a memento of the occasion or as proof of the affair, the DNA on it proved her soul mate had a definite physical dimension much to the chagrin of his administration and the mortification of his wife. The blue dress conferred instant, albeit dubious, celebrity on Lewinsky for a very long political season.

What star of the reality TV reality show *Teen Mom* decided that prison time was the best option for her to get her out-of-control life back together in 2012?

A teen mom at 16, Amber Portman rocketed to reality show fame for nothing more than getting pregnant, having a baby, and being on MTV's *Teen Mom*, a spin-off of *16 and Pregnant*. Her problems with addiction were highlighted on the show as well as her obnoxious behavior.

Amber made another in a seemingly unending series of bad choices when she dropped out of a court-ordered rehab program and opted for a stint in prison rather than taking another stab at getting clean and sober on the outside.

Amber's rationale for choosing prison was that she would finally be able to get her GED and could do her rehab there. She reportedly now regrets that decision. But not to worry, the show's producers will probably figure out how to do a reality show about her jailbird days. *Teen Mom in Jail* sounds like a good start.

We all know babies are adorable but the exhaustive exploitation of this subject is not and neither is the cast of characters paraded out on these shows. That a teenager's pregnancy could be the qualifier for making an Instant Celebrity out of nobody boggles any reasonable mind.

News Flash:

There is now a new installment of a baby-based reality show called *My Teen is Pregnant and So Am I.* TLC's new offering follows several mother-daughter duos through their pregnancies to their deliveries while comparing their baby bumps along the way.

In one of the episodes teen mom-to-be, Liz Forbes, complains about her mother stealing her thunder by being pregnant at the same time as she is. In fact, Liz thought it was selfish of her mom since she and her own baby would no longer be receiving all the attention. Whatever, the self-centered, self-seeking Liz will still get oodles of attention from fans who love this stuff.

The Instant Celebrity

Who was George Jorgensen and what turned him into an overnight sensation in the early 1950s?

He was the first ex-GI to become a real lady. In 1952 George went to Denmark and returned as Christine Jorgensen, a veteran of one of the first sex-change operations to be performed on an American man. The new lady became an Instant Celebrity who caused a media furor, not only in the United States, but throughout the world.

What "escort" achieve instant notoriety when she had a dust-up with a member of the Secret Service?

A young Colombian woman called Dania Saurez. Her star was launched into the Instant Celebrity firmament when she took on a secret service agent after he refused to pay her what they had been agreed upon earlier for her services.

Being that prostitution is legal in Colombia the complaining woman wasted no time in taking her grievances to the police who then notified American authorities. Dania told the press that had she been a spy wanting to obtain "sensitive information" from the agent it wouldn't have been difficult. She claimed that during their tête-à-tête, or whatever you want to call it, she had access to the agent's wallet while he was passed out from an alcohol-induced stupor.

Emboldened by her new found fame, Dania put it out there that she would consider doing a nude layout for the right magazine and the right paycheck. It is obvious

Dania knows how to take full advantage of her 15 minutes before, poof, it's gone.

Who parachuted out of a jet plane over Oregon in 1971 with a big bundle of ransom money and became a never-to-be-heard-from-again Instant Celebrity?

A man, now folk hero, called Dan Cooper. D.B. Cooper as he is most often referred to, boarded a Northwest Orient flight from Portland to Seattle in the winter of 1971.

Once on the plane Cooper put on a pair of sunglasses, ordered a drink, and handed the stewardess a note reading, "I have a bomb in my suitcase. I will use it if necessary. I want you to sit next to me. You are being hijacked."

The captain was then notified that Cooper wanted $200,000 and some parachutes once they landed in

Seattle. As a good will gesture in exchange for the money, he would allow the passengers to disembark. The FBI was notified and complied with Cooper's demands.

Once the plane was up in the air again, sans passengers, the skyjacker ordered the Captain to maintain an altitude under 10,000 feet and release plane's rear stairs. Cooper then jumped out of the jet and was never seen or heard from again. Many believe he was killed in the jump or may have died from exposure as it was a very cold, stormy night. Whatever the case, some of the ransom bills intermittently show up along the Columbia River. Of course, there are the off-and-on alleged sightings of D.B. Cooper. The only ones you can trust, however, are those of him on tee shirts celebrating his exploit.

Is there really a reality show about virgins?

Need you even ask? There are apparently still a few women out there past the age of 18 who seem more than willing and are ready to flaunt it on *The Virgin Diaries*. In TLC's series three virgins are featured who talk you and everyone else silly with their chasteness. Whatever, it is giving virtue a chance at the spotlight and the producers, a fistful of cash for cleverly sexualizing it.

Go figure. It seems that if you can't sing or dance, or have any other marketable talent, your ace in the hole, so to speak, is your virginity, at least in the case of this reality show.

Who famously said of fame that it was "The advantage of being known by people of whom you yourself know nothing, and for whom you care as little"?

Poet Lord Byron aka George Noel Gordon. He said it over 200 years ago. Today's Instant Celebrities, for the most part, could care even less for the fawning masses that made them famous for 15 minutes.

What U.S. Senator's scandalous toe-tapping behavior soft-shoed him right out of office?

Idaho's republican senator, Larry Craig, who on June 11, 2007, was arrested at the Minneapolis-St. Paul International Airport for allegedly soliciting an undercover officer from his bathroom stall with some fancy footwork. Senator Craig inserted his foot into the adjacent stall and tapped his shoe – a "code" said to be used by some gays for "are you interested?" Whatever, it didn't work.

The undercover police cop then arrested Craig on suspicion of lewd conduct. The Senator, of course, denied his arrestor's version of events saying that he had a "wide stance" being that he was a "wide guy" and that he had merely been picking something up off the floor. How he planned to do that with his shoed foot was never made clear.

Following the incident Craig, who has been the proponent of anti-gay legislation, said he was totally innocent of the charge but did plead guilty to a misdemeanor of disorderly conduct. The senator held a press conference several months later and said he realized he should not have pleaded as he did.

His attorneys tried to have his guilty plea withdrawn arguing that it "was not knowing and intelligent and therefore was in violation of his constitutional rights." Whatever the legal verbiage meant to accomplish, it didn't work and Craig's motion was denied.

Craig held a news conference and promised to resign,

then changed his mind saying he would serve out his term as he needed time to clear his name in the Senate Ethic's Committee. Craig did finish out his term but wisely did not seek reelection in 2008, no doubt realizing the electorate would never forgive him his 15 minutes of shoe-tapping notoriety.

What unfortunate shooting accident turned Harry Whittington into an instant, but quite reluctant, 15-minute celebrity?

Poor Harry became an unwanted sound byte when Vice President Cheney shot him in the face with a shotgun while the two were on a hunting trip. Perhaps in the fog of the moment Cheney mistook him for the duck he was hoping to bag. Any other explanation seems almost as improbable.

The lead pellets pierced Whittington's larynx and he has warbled ever since. (Who could resist the pun?) The birdshot also winged his hand and pelted his right forehead where tiny lead bumps remain embedded as souvenirs of Cheney's errant aim.

Whittington's memory of being shot by the vice president is hazy. He only recalls that after getting a whiff of burning powder, he keeled over in a dead faint. His injuries led to down time in the hospital and a lot of up time on news and talk shows, especially the late night ones where he was endlessly satirized.

Now inextricably linked with the Vice President Cheney, Whittington cannot escape the fickle finger of fate's most dreaded designation – executive folly in the duck blinds.

Who gained instant notoriety when he confessed to an infamous crime he did not commit?

John Mark Karr. In 2006 he was arrested in Thailand after falsely confessing to the 1996 slaying of Jon Benet Ramsey, the popular beauty queen tot. Apparently, a pathological need for attention is what drives people like Karr and others like him to claim ownership of crimes they didn't commit. Some speculate in Karr's case his rich fantasy life about Jon Benet Ramsey – he claimed he loved her – caused him to lose hold on reality.

In any case Karr was soon released from jail as the police questioning confirmed he was not the murderer of Jon Benet Ramsey. Though surprising as it might seem, there was nothing Karr could be charged with at the time – not even his love confession or obvious pedophiliac tendencies. But his sick need for attention got him what he was after. His picture was plastered on every media outlet around the world for an uncomfortably long 15 minutes.

Note: The strange can always get stranger. After being arrested in a domestic dust-up with a girlfriend in Georgia in 2008, John Mark Karr dropped out of sight and resurfaced on the web several years later as Alexis Valoran Reich and/or Delia Alexis Reich after reportedly having a sex change operation. Maybe as Alexis, she figures there is yet another 15 minutes to be had.

What woman famously declined Marlon Brando's 1973 Oscar for Best Actor in *The Godfather* at the 45th Academy Awards?

A Native American called Sacheen Littlefeather. Brando and Littlefeather used his Oscar to make a statement about the infamous 1973 Wounded Knee incident and to voice their objections about how Native Americans were being depicted in the movies and on TV at the time. When Brando's name was announced at the award ceremony, Littlefeather, in full Apache dress, went on stage and refused the Oscar, saying she was doing so on his behalf.

The incident caused audible gasps and made an Instant Celebrity of Sacheen Littlefeather. This was the first time anyone had ever used Oscar as a political statement* while simultaneously shunning the award's acknowledgment of a nominee's celebrity and talent. After the award show, Littlefeather held a news conference voicing everything she wasn't allowed to say during the award show.

* George C. Scott refused his Oscar in 1970 but did so, not as a political statement, but because he wanted the Academy and others to know that he did not believe in a competition with fellow nominees.

Note: In 1973 members of AIM (American Indian Movement) occupied the town of Wounded Knee, South Dakota, for 71 days. The confrontation between the U.S. government and about 200 Oglala Lakota ended in two dead Native Americans and one FBI agent.

What man became famous overnight as the result of a savage beating at the hands of the LAPD following a high-speed car case?

Rodney King. The minute a video of the 1991 incident was shown on television, there was widespread condemnation of the horrific beating. When the police officers indicted for assaulting him were subsequently acquitted at trial, Los Angeles exploded into some of deadliest riots in U.S. history. Countless buildings and property were torched all over the city coming to an estimated one billion dollars in damage and, before it was over, 50 people were killed and some 2,000 injured.

In an ironic twist, after surviving the savage beating and the riots that followed, Rodney King drowned in his home swimming pool in June, 2012. In an interview with National Public Radio shortly before his death King said he would like the following to appear on his headstone: "Can we all just get along? Can we all get along in peace?" They are the same words ones he plaintively uttered into the television camera after his beating.

Who became an instant folk hero when he deployed the plane's emergency chute, grabbed a beer, and made a sliding exit out of a job he just could not stand any more?

Jet Blue career flight attendant Steven Slater. After an argument with a passenger who refused to apologize after her overhead luggage beaned him on the head, Slater got on the intercom and purged all his pent-up years of job stress and abuse with a string of well-aimed curses at his offender. The flight attendant then declared, almost as an aside, "It's been great!" – and with that parting salvo, jumped ship and took off down the tarmac into welcomed unemployment.

Mr. Slater was charged with criminal mischief and reckless endangerment but not before everyone who was fed up with their own job commiserated by tweeting and facebooking their support of his actions. Mr. Slater didn't do any jail time but did pay a fine and had to submit to a mental health evaluation.

Though people may no longer recall Steven Slater's name, many of them will no doubt remember a flight attendant who one day gave the world his very public version of "Take This Job and Shove It."

What reality star has been called "America's most beloved piece of Italian trash"?

Nicole "Snooki" Polizzi of *Jersey Shore*. Trash-talking, cat-fighting, hard-partying, hard-drinking Snooki is at the top of a very long list of people who have seized their 15 minutes for little more than knowing how to behave badly.

After five long seasons on *Jersey Shore* her mouthy, frequently over-the-top, and out-of-control behavior was rewarded by MTV with a spin-off reality show called *Snooki and JWOWW* which debuted in the summer of 2012.

Snooki began taping the new show while pregnant and said she didn't want to marry the child's father until her baby could be at the wedding ceremony. The baby might skyrocket ratings of the new show and then, of course, the pending marriage to and/or split from her beau (you never know which it might be) could do so as well. Recently asked about her thoughts on child rearing, Snooki replied that when her child finally saw an episode of *Jersey Shore* she would simply tell the kid, "this is what not to do."

Who knows? Snookie could have the last laugh and extend her 15 minutes if her stated wish comes true – that she would like to do reality shows until she's 90. Yikes!

What other-worldly event turned Travis Walton into an Instant Celebrity one November night in 1975?

His abduction by aliens. Returning home from work on the night of November 5, 1975, Walton and several other men saw what they claimed was a UFO in the Sitgreaves National Forest a short distance outside of Snowflake, Arizona. Curious about the hovering craft, Walton got out the pickup over the objections of the others and approached it. When he did, a beam of light from the spaceship knocked him unconscious.

The men he was with panicked and left the scene, not knowing whether Walton was dead or alive. One of them returned later but couldn't find Walton anywhere. The sheriff interviewed the bunch and initiated a murder investigation even though the suspects had supposedly passed lie detector tests at the time.

Five days later Travis Walton showed up butt naked at a gas station, delirious and dehydrated. During a later flashback he described being probed by awful-looking creatures with scary, dark, luminous eyes. Walton also submitted to a lie detector test and passed.

Local officials, as well as others who came to Snowflake to examine the men, considered the whole story a hoax but were at loss to explain the mirror image accounts of the men's stories and how they had passed their polygraphs. They were either all good at deception, suffering from mass hysteria or, perhaps, they really did see something that rattled their psyches. Whatever it was, the men did not budge from their account of that night's events.

Travis Walton's new found celebrity got him lots of tabloid attention as well as a novel and even a movie deal. The film about his abduction, *Fire in the Sky*, came out in 1993. The crawl at the end says all the men involved in the UFO sighting once again resubmitted to polygraphs that same year and passed. They believe the tests should prove once and for all they were telling the truth.

What e-mail invitation got a British call center employee dismissed from her job and brought her the kind of instant media coverage some wannabe celebrities can only dream about?

In 2002 Rachel Fountain accidentally e-mailed an invitation for a porno-themed gathering to her boss's inbox, a finance director at American Express. After being fired, Rachel was hardly cowed or contrite about the incident. In fact, she wasted no time in writing about it on online. A local journalist saw the posting and asked her for an interview. When the larger media picked that up, Rachel's story went viral.

Murdock's *News of the World* offered her a handsome paycheck for yet another accounting of the blowback caused by her notorious e-mail invitation. Before all was said and done, Rachel was invited to pose in her underwear for even more compensation. She was enjoying every minute of her 15 in the celebrity spotlight.

To think an erroneously sent invite could cause so much ado about nothing and be the reason a simple nobody could get 15 minutes of lucrative, short-lived fame is difficult to fathom. It appears that nothing succeeds like bravado and good old self-promotion.

What author's "memoir," *A Million Little Pieces*, made Oprah's Book Club pick in 2005 only to be later ignominiously demoted off the list?

James Frey's. In the wake of heated media coverage as to the memoir's veracity, Oprah had Frey come back on the show and address the accusations about his reputed life as a criminal and addict which he detailed in the book. She pointedly asked him whether or not he had actually spent time in jail. He had not. She also wanted to know if his story about having two root canals without anesthesia was true. It was not. In his "memoir" Frey described the root canals in agonizing detail and said the reason he had suffered the procedures with no anesthesia was because – you probably guessed it - he was an addict and couldn't take painkillers lest they might put him back on the slippery slope of addiction.

Frey's admissions were slow in coming and when they finally came, it looked like Oprah could have torn her book club pick into a million little pieces right along with its author.

Frey later tried to rehabilitate his image by making the rounds on the talk show circuit stressing how all memoirs are embellished. You take some truth and embroider it with a little bit of interesting this and that – no harm done. In Frey's case though, he seems to have taken one huge fib after another and stitched in a modicum of truth until he ended up with a notorious bit of literary feint and sham he claimed as a memoir. So much for his brief moment in Oprah's limelight.

What well respected 65-year old college professor was outed in a sting operation as a transsexual prostitute?

Max Reinhart aka "Sasha." The secondary career of the well regarded University of Georgia professor went viral in 2012 when "she" was caught accepting money for sex. Reinhart used the internet to promote himself as a "transsexual escort." One wonders how he managed to drum up any business as "Sasha" since this alter ego was not a particularly fetching sight.

In any event the unfortunate professor was jailed then released on bail after which he released a statement saying he was sorry about the whole thing. He didn't want his moonlighting activities to reflect adversely on the University of Georgia.

What creator of television's first "reality show" made him instantly famous and forever notorious?

In the early 70s Craig Gilbert pitched the idea for a television series to PBS called *An American Family*. The starring role eventually went to the Loud Family of Santa Barbara, California, and chronicled the day-to-day life of Bill and Pat Loud and their five children. Filmed over seven months in 1971 the series ended with the Louds filing for a divorce and a houseful of miserable, upset kids.

When *An American Family* finally aired in 1973, it proved to be a ratings bonanza mostly because it was not the Norman Rockwell version the viewing audience expected. Instead it exposed the kind of difficulties and secrets most families kept away from prying eyes of others including their own marital problems and one of their son's flamboyant gayness.

The Loud Family was so upset with their negative depiction in the series they all went on "The Dick Cavett Show," a popular talk show in the 70s, and accused Craig Gilbert of cherry picking his 300 hours of film footage and then editing it to show them in the worst possible light. The family claimed they had no idea the show would cause them such personal and public grief and change their lives the way it did. In short, what they thought they signed up for was not what Gilbert had represented when he originally approached them to do the show.

While Loud family ultimately survived the personal upheavals caused by the reality show (Bill and Pat even remarried), Craig Gilbert did not fare as well. He never worked again. The Loud family's PR campaign, as well as assertions made by Gilbert's own staff, successfully cast him as a Svengali who would do anything and everything to get what he wanted on film no matter whom it hurt. This sounds a bit like the people who produce today's reality shows but without the punitive blowback.

Note: In 2011 HBO aired *Cinema Verite* with Diane Lane and Tim Robbins playing Pat and Bill Loud. The docudrama reenacted the 1971 filming of *An American Family* and included the Louds' behind-the-scenes meetings with Craig Gilbert leading up to doing the PBS series as well as their many tense meetings with him during the show's production.

What winner of the first *Survivor* reality show saw instant fame quickly turn into notoriety when he went to jail?

Richard Hatch. The former corporate trainer, bartender and car salesman was the winner of CBS' first season of the reality TV series *Survivor: Borneo*. He is all too remembered as a contentious, conniving, cocky contestant who chose to do much of the series butt naked. He frequently rubbed his rival survivalists the wrong way and toward the end of the show one contestant wasted no love and no words, referring to him as a snake.

Notwithstanding the many negative opinions other competitors had about Hatch, he was voted the first Sole Survivor on the show and went on to appear in a follow-up series called *Survivor: All Stars*, again participating in the buff much to the annoyance of several other contestants.

After Hatch was voted off the last series, he extended his 15 minutes a tad longer doing other reality shows including the *Battle of the Network Reality Shows* and Australia's *Who Wants to Be a Millionaire,* to mention a few.

His celebrity lost most of its luster after he was convicted of tax evasion and sentenced to prison several different times. In each case Hatch declared his innocence on all counts saying the charges of which he had been convicted were baseless – that he had been unfairly targeted by the government.

Whatever the case, Hatch seems hungry for another 15 minutes and in the summer of 2012, hinted that another show was in the offing.

Who was dubbed the "Preppie Killer" and why?

Robert Chambers was so-called because of his tall, handsome good looks, and once promising collegiate future. The press stuck him with epithet after he killed Jennifer Levin in Central Park on August 26, 1986. Before being booked into jail he told his father, "That fucking bitch, why didn't she leave me alone?" The preppie charmer used the "rough sex defense" for his trial claiming Levin's death was an accident, the result of sex play getting out of control and his ultimately having to defend himself against her aggressive advances.

49

While out on bail Chambers was filmed strangling a doll in what has come to be called the "Barbie" video. In the clip he is seen with several scantily clad women who watch him as he first chokes himself while making loud gagging noises then twists off the doll's head as he says in a mocking, high-pitched voice, "My name is… Oops! I think I killed it."

If ever there were a narcissistic sociopath, Robert Chambers easily wins the distinction. Why the media felt no compunction about making him into an Instant Celebrity is another story. But his mug was plastered on the front page of many newspapers across the country for many months and television featured endless stories about him. He was obviously the stuff of tabloid heaven. Only after he went to prison did his hellish celebrity finally wane.

What Wall Street big shot's ponzi scheme bilked billions out of investors, charities, and even his own friends?

Bernie Madoff's. He was a stockbroker, financier and financial advisor to the wealthy and was perceived as a sort of Wall Street money God, repeatedly making high returns on investors' money. In fact, people actually begged him to invest for them believing his Midas touch would reap big profits for them.

Ultimately though, perception didn't match reality and when the banking crisis hit in 2008, Madoff couldn't keep his game up. With few new investors and others needing their money out of his investment firm Madoff knew his ponzi* scheme couldn't be sustained.

When Madoff's money pyramid finally collapsed, many people were left penniless and some investors who had believed he was the real deal committed suicide after their losses. Even one of his sons killed himself – some say more from shame and depression than his relative penury after the big fall. Though Madoff's two sons worked for the company, they both claimed to have had no knowledge of what their father was doing.

Almost overnight Bernie Madoff went from being a celebrated money maker to a despised, notorious crook. He was convicted and sentenced to a jillion years in prison where he shall no doubt end his days contemplating how the rich and famous can quickly become the poor and infamous.

* A Ponzi scheme is a con that promises to pay exorbitant returns to investors. The money paid to them

is obtained from an ever increasing number of new investors which ultimately dries up and leaves the last ones in holding an empty bag with a painful look of desperation on their faces.

What American born woman went from being an actress to a famous Nazi propagandist to teaching kindergarten?

Mildred Gillers aka "Axis Sally." After a tepid career as an actress in the 1920s, Gillers left the United States to seek fame abroad. She found it doing shortwave English radio broadcasts in Germany extolling the virtues of Hitler's Third Reich for all within earshot. Arrested and tried for treason, Gillers was sentenced to prison.

She was paroled in 1961 and repaired to Ohio where she spent her remaining years as a kindergarten teacher. "Axis Sally" never apologized for her part in disseminating propaganda against the Allies during World War II and, in fact, is said to have remained a steadfast admirer of the Nazis. After all, they had turned her from a complete nobody into a big international celebrity – albeit a very notorious one.

What string of reality shows feature wives, relatives, etc., of the mob?

There are a slew of them and the shows have proven a vehicle for much Instant Celebrity. The reality show, *Growing Up Gotti*, featured Victoria Gotti, daughter of John Gotti, the Gambino family's one time mobster boss.

Then there's *Mob Wives* and *"Big Ang,"* the latter starring Angela "Big Ang" Raiola, the niece of Salvatore "Sally Dogs" Lombardi who once captained the Genovese crime family.

Big Ang is unapologetic about her connection to the mob, indeed she revels in it. She has many fans and a bunch of websites devoted to her. Invited on *The View* in July, 2012, the likeable and charismatic Big Ang told the women on the show she loved dating "Wiseguys" (street hoodlums) in her youth because they knew how to treat a woman, lavishing expensive gifts and many a good time on her. Big Ang also said she loved being in the Instant Celebrity spotlight – not that you could tell, modest and retiring soul that she is.

So it is. To be in any way associated with the mafia these days is a connection that can get you 15 minutes of fame. Once shunned by so-called law abiding society, popular culture now embraces Wiseguys and all those who know how to capitalize on their linkage to them.

What teenager stole guns, boats, planes, and just about anything else that was not nailed down, while successfully managing to elude federal authorities for several years?

Colton Harris-Moore aka the "Barefoot Bandit," so called because he once left 39 chalked barefoot prints at the scene of a crime with the departing taunt, "C'ya!" Not exactly John Greenleaf Whittier's "barefoot boy, with cheeks of tan," Colton's ne'er-do-well life of crime nonetheless charmed many and he had a big following on the internet rooting for him as the ultimate outlaw – young, daring, inventive, smart and cocky – and one who always managed to escape authorities.

Though his stealing spree began in the Northwest where he was born and lived, it came to an end in July, 2010, at the ripe old age of 19, after he stole a plane and flew to the Bahamas where he crash landed it on Great Abaco Island. Several days later, while once again trying to elude law enforcement, the police managed to shoot out the engine of a motorboat he was using in yet another escape attempt. In 2012 the "Barefoot Bandit" was sentenced to six-and-a-half years and his artful career in crime came to an abrupt end – for the time being anyway.

Of course, as with any Instant Celebrity, there is always a book. This one is called *The Barefoot Bandit: The True Tale of Colton Harris-Moore*.

Who claimed he rescued Howard Hughes lying on the side of a road in the Nevada desert in 1967?

Melvin Dummar. His story, who few people believe, was nonetheless later made into a movie called *Melvin and Howard*. The tale of the lost millionaire goes something like this.

Melvin, who was a gas station attendant, found the scruffy Hughes lying along a lonely stretch of highway in the Nevada desert. He picked Hughes up and took him back to the Sands Hotel in Las Vegas where the millionaire lived at the time. According to Dummar, Hughes did not reveal who he was until he was about to be dropped off at the Sands.

How and why Hughes got stranded in the middle of the desert was never credibly explained by Dummar but his association with the millionaire, invented or not, made him an Instant Celebrity just by virtue of his implied connection to him.

When Howard Hughes died, Dummar contested the millionaire's will by providing the most byzantine of explanations as to how $156 million had supposedly been left to him. He said one night a man showed up at his gas station with an envelope and instructed Melvin to deliver it to the headquarters of The Church of Latter Day Saints which, it seems, had also been left a chunk of money by Hughes. The "Mormon Will," as it was later known, was ultimately ruled a forgery by the courts.

Apparently, Dummar's wife was an enterprising and inventive soul who had access to lots of information on

Hughes while working for a magazine called *Millionaire*. The publication was a favorite of the wealthy and its subscriber database gave Mrs. Dummar much privileged information, including Hughes's.

Mrs. Dummar denied forging the will and, for what ever reason, no criminal charges were brought against her or her husband. The Dummars, for all their cunning, did not get a nickel of the Hughes estate.

What happened to one Phineas Gage that should have killed him straight away, but instead turned him into an Instant Celebrity who is still remembered in medical circles over 150 years later?

An explosion in a Cavendish, Vermont railroad yard in 1848 shot a three-and-a-half-foot iron rod, measuring one-and-a-quarter inches in diameter and weighing over 10 pounds, through his cheek then up through the front of his brain and out the top of his head. The iron rod landed some one hundred feet away.

According to accounts of the incident, Phineas remained conscious afterward and was even able to walk around and talk coherently. Except for a blinded left eye, Phineas was pronounced physically cured of his wound several months later. His personality, however, took a sharp turn. Phineas wasn't so agreeable anymore.

What 34-year old, very attractive school teacher went to jail for having an affair with her grade school pupil and then later married him?

Mary Kay Letourneau. She had two children by Vili Fualauu, her former middle school pupil and lover. After serving more than seven years for child molesting, Letourneau got out of prison in 2004 and later married Fualaau.

The teacher claims nothing and no one could have kept them apart - that her connection with Fualaau is "endless and eternal." For his part, in an interview on *Inside Edition*, Fualaau stated that he did not believe himself to be a victim and declared his love for his former school teacher.

When Letourneau met Fualaau she was a 34-year old married mother of four living in Seattle. She became pregnant by Fualauu with their first child when he was still only 13. A book about their relationship, *Only One Crime, Love*, was later co-authored by the two lovebirds and released in France. The controversy surrounding the pair turned them both into Instant Celebrities who were momentarily notorious for flaunting not only convention, but the law as well.

Whose much publicized 25-minute walk across the Niagara Falls brought instantaneous celebrity to an enterprising daredevil?

Nik Wallenda's. The offspring of the well-known daredevil Wallenda family, few knew of Nik until he walked a tightrope two-inches in diameter and some 1,800 feet long - about the length of six football fields - across the Niagara Falls to Canada on June 15, 2012.

Wallenda later said in one of countless interviews that he had thought about attempting this feat his whole life and had trained for it accordingly so he could deal with the spray, wind, and other challenges of the long crossing. He also said the daring walk was, in part, a tribute to his great-grandfather, Karl Wallenda, who died in 1978 when he fell off a high wire stretched between two buildings in Puerto Rico.

Nic Wallenda's stunt was a ratings gold mine for the

media and focused worldwide celebrity on the high-wire walker who promised his next act would be even grander – the Grand Canyon, in fact. He is said to already have the necessary permits for this next stunt.

Some reporters tried to downplay Nik Wallenda's accomplishment by pointing to the safety harness he had worn while crossing the Falls. NBC and CTV apparently required him to wear it as the television channels did not want him falling to his death on live TV. The daredevil supposedly told his dad "he felt like a jackass" with it on. Though some thought he might even take the harness off once he started his harrowing walk, he didn't.

Who knows? Maybe Wallenda will attempt the Grand Canyon crossing without the benefit of a safety wire if he can convince the media to go along with him. While such an audacious stunt would skyrocket viewer ratings, the perception of it as skewing safety would be problematic for media outlets. Ergo, it probably won't happen.

The Instant Celebrity

What philosopher and poet said "The highest form of vanity is love of fame"?

George Santayana. Just get one of today's Instant Celebrities to understand what Santayana meant by those words. It would probably be impossible. Vainglory is the Instant Celebrity's middle name.

Who made the 24/7 news cycle for many weeks as the most famous party crashers in U.S. history?

Michaele & Tareq Salahi. They successfully crashed a party at the White House in 2009 without being detected by the Secret Service. The stunt was reportedly a bid to get their own reality show. While at the party the interlopers sidled up next to President Obama for a photo op and a little tête-à-tête before moving on to other dignitaries at the gala Whitehouse dinner. The nervy couple later posted pictures of themselves at the event on Facebook.

In an appearance on the *Today Show* the Salahis remained adamant they had been invited to the White House party – that any perception to the contrary was simply a misunderstanding. It subsequently came out that the couple had also invited themselves to other Washington social functions as well, including an awards dinner for the Congressional Black Caucus Foundation at which President Obama spoke.

The Salahis managed to parlay all their party crashing into a lot of ink and television time and short-lived attempts at reality TV. As accomplished imposters they were never quite able to overcome the creep-factor associated with their antics and their name has since become synonymous with an unwelcome or uninvited guest. Now divorced, Micaele and Tareq will have to party crash alone or find another willing accomplice.

What epithet was used to describe the most famous whistleblower in American history?

Deep Throat. William Mark Felt, an FBI agent, was the anonymous source for *The Washington Post* coverage of the infamous 1972 break-in at the Watergate Hotel in Washington, D. C. The ensuing scandal led to President Richard Nixon's resignation.

Even when Felt's identity was finally revealed in 2005 his celebrity appeal never matched that of his anonymous alter ego, Deep Throat. Apparently, the mystery and intrigue of the name had star power and sold papers like crazy since it had kept people guessing about whom Bernstein and Woodward's source might possibly be.

Some speculate the use of name Deep Throat was because Bernstein and Woodward met with Felt on the bottom level of a dark underground garage - conjuring up deep cover so to speak. Or, who knows, maybe the reporters just had a sense of humor. *Deep Throat* was also the name of a popular porno film at the time for reasons not so hard to conjure up.

Note: A book called *All the President's Men* by Carl Bernstein and Bob Woodward told the story of the Watergate scandal in exhausting detail. The book won them the Pulitzer Prize for investigative journalism.

What videographer became instantly famous when her affair with presidential hopeful John Edwards appeared in the tabloids?

Rielle Hunter. Not only did she have an affair with the former senator and vice presidential candidate, she was secretly pregnant with his child during the 2008 campaign. The cheating and cover-up that followed contributed to Edwards's failed candidacy and Rielle's vilification as "the other woman." At the time Elizabeth Edwards, the candidate's wife, was fighting cancer.

John Edwards denied he was the father of Rielle's Hunter's child on national television, saying a paternity test would prove it. He later reportedly called Rielle several choice epithets. In the end, *The National*

Enquirer proved him a liar when it printed pictures of Edwards holding his child.

Rielle Hunter's book, *What Really Happened: John Edwards, Our Daughter, and Me,* came hot off the press in 2012 explaining that she was neither the villain the press had made her out to be nor was Elizabeth Edwards, the saint. Notwithstanding the truth or falsehood in this unfortunate story, Rielle has parlayed her and everyone else's misery into fame and fortune.

What did Barack Obama say about his 15 minutes of fame?

The President said "The fact that my 15 minutes of fame has extended a little longer than 15 minutes is somewhat surprising to me and completely baffling to my wife."

What charismatic preacher man held such sway over his flock they all drank poisoned Kool-Aid for him?

Jim Jones, head of the People's Temple in Jonestown, British Guyana. After Leo Ryan, a California congressman, went down to South America as part of a government investigation to see what was going on in Jonestown, the preacher became more paranoid and unhinged than he already was. He didn't want the government poking around in his town.

One reason Ryan had gone to Guyana was to see if any members of the People's Temple were being held against their will as some of their stateside relatives believed. In the view of some, Jonestown had become a spiritual "gulag" where church members were no longer free to do as they pleased.

While Leo Ryan was at Jonestown, his interaction with its leader became increasingly tense. As a result, the congressman decided to cut short his trip and return to the States with a few People's Temple members who wanted to leave the commune. When Ryan and his returning party later attempted to board a nearby plane, they were machine gunned down by cult loyalists.

After the massacre, the ever more erratic and delusional Jones told his followers about what had happened at the airstrip and how now they would never be left alone to practice their religion. He then convinced his flock to sacrifice their lives for their church.

On November 17, 1977, over 900 of them drank a

poisoned purple concoction that included cyanide and sedatives, and soon expired under the hot Jonestown sun. Jim Jones would have none of the Kool-Aid himself. He ended his life with a bullet.

No mass suicide has ever made the impression or had quite the news traction this story did. As well, few so-called men of God have ever achieved such instant notoriety.

What actress turned nun is still an Oscar-voting member of the Academy of Motion Picture Arts and Sciences?

Delores Hart aka Reverend Mother Delores Hart, a Benedictine nun, is once again enjoying 15 minutes with a whole new persona. Hollywood's darling in the 1960s, Hart had a successful run of it in tinsel town including doing two pictures in which she starred with Elvis Presley, *Loving You* and *King Creole*. She denied ever having an affair with Elvis but when asked how it felt to kiss him on screen the Reverend Mother answered with a quiet laugh, "I think the limit for a screen kiss back then was something like 15 seconds. That one has lasted 40 years."

Hart attended the 2012 Academy Awards personally. A documentary about her life called *God is the Bigger Elvis* was in contention for an Oscar but didn't win. Her last trip down the red carpet before then was back in 1959. She seemed to relish the Instant Celebrity her habit afforded her more than she did her stint in Hollywood as a starlet.

What pop-and-dance team's extraordinary overnight success in the late 80s won them a Grammy Award which was later revoked for fraud?

Milli Vanilli, the group formed by Fab Morvan and Rob Pilatus. Their debut album, *All or Nothing*, as it was called in Europe and, *Girl You Know It's True*, as it was renamed for stateside release, brought them instant international fame and fortune as well the 1990 Grammy Award for Best New Artist. Their Grammy was later taken back when it was discovered the lead vocals on their album were not the actual voices of the attractive pop duo, but those of talented unknowns.

When the energetic Milli Vanilli duo performed on stage, they simply lip synced the anonymous singers' voices while dancing up a storm and no one was the wiser, at least not for a while - right up to the moment when they were outed as the biggest frauds in music history.

After the uproar from the scandal quieted down, the two released an album singing in their own voices called *The Real Milli Vanilli.*   However, it never met with success.   In 1998 Rob Pilatus was found dead of an apparent overdose in Frankfurt, Germany.   His partner, Fab Morvan, tried to go it solo he but never quite made it.

Milli Vanilli is a sadly cautionary tale of Instant Celebrity instantly interrupted.   To this day the name, Milli Vanilli, is still used in many quarters to describe something that is fraudulent - a meme for deception and fakery.

Why did giving birth to a baby make Lesley Brown very famous for 15 minutes?

Her baby was the first "test tube baby," one conceived by in vitro fertilization. The 1978 birth of her daughter, Louise, made headlines all over the world for many news cycles. Now people don't even remember who Lesley Brown was. She died in 2012.

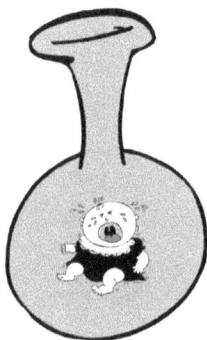

What groupie girl pack got their 15 minutes simply for catching a tiger by the tail and hanging on until their lawyers showed up?

Rachel Uchitel, Jamie Grubbs and Jamie Jungers are just a few on a long list of now forgotten women who dated and/or slept with and/or whatever with the world's then premier golfer, Tiger Woods. His indiscretions and their desire for compensation, mostly lawyered under the table, led to a very public scandal for the golfer, embarrassment and humiliation for his wife, and lots of publicity for everyone else.

When Tiger's wife, Elin Nordegren, found out about the extent of his philandering, she supposedly went ballistic and chased out him of their Florida home wielding a golf club. Whatever may or may not have happened in the wee morning hours that November in 2009, Tiger did run into a tree backing out of his driveway. However, while the tree didn't smash out the Cadillac Escalade's back window, it is speculated that a golf club may have.

Following the marital dust-up, the duffer's wife divorced him and returned to Sweden. Tiger's game on the golf course has not been quite the same since. Who knows about off? Unfortunately for him, he is now more famous in many people's minds as a serial adulterer than as one of the best golfers ever.

To what did Peg Enwhistle, an aspiring actress in the 1930s, owe her dubious celebrity?

She committed suicide off the HOLLYWOOD sign. Initial rumors had her jumping off the 13th letter – at the time the sign read: HOLLYWOODLAND – seemingly a pitiful last reference to a bit part the actress played in her only film, *Thirteen Women*. Peg, however, did nothing so creatively cryptic. She was just resourceful. She climbed up a workman's ladder that had been left behind the "H" and dove off, instantly seizing the 15 minutes which had eluded her in life.

What man became an overnight celebrity when his wife cut off his penis and threw it away?

John Wayne Bobbitt. Yep, it's true. Mr. Bobbitt had his penis bobbed by his wife, Lorena, and the incident made him an Instant Celebrity. It just goes to show you, you can be become famous for anything - even losing your penis, well temporarily anyway. This unusual story that happened in 1993 has an even more unusual ending.

Lorena, in a fit of rage after her husband supposedly physically abused her, whacked off his penis and made a quick getaway with it, finally tossing the former object of her affection out a car window. Luckily for Bobbitt, his wife felt enough remorse to call 911. An extensive search was launched and the discarded member was recovered while it could still be surgically reattached.

The operation was apparently a complete success. A year later, Mr. Bobbitt starred in an X-rated flick that demanded his very best and he gave it, extending, as it were, his 15 minutes.

What respected headmistress of an exclusive girl's school in Virginia shot and killed her internationally famous doctor lover?

Jean Harris. In 1980 Harris shot the famous diet doctor, Dr. Herman Tarnower, three times at his New York mansion. She was quickly apprehended by the police and denied it had ever been her intent to kill the good doctor when she went to see him.

Author of the celebrated *The Complete Scarsdale Medical Diet*, Tarnower's murder stunned the world especially since it had been at the hands of the very prim and proper Jean Harris, headmistress of the elite Madeira School for girls. The press attributed Harris's motive to jealousy as it was well known that Tarnower had many lovers – a fact Ms. Harris may have been unaware of or, in her swoon for the doctor, initially ignored.

A lifelong bachelor, Tarnower said he was married to his profession. Quite the charmer, he liked the ladies and they obviously liked him back. He once quipped, "I'm thinking of throwing a party and inviting all the women who are chasing me." It seems Harris got tired of the chase and accidentally, or not, brought Romeo to ground.

Tarnower's homicide made Harris a notorious Instant Celebrity and got her sentenced to prison where she spent many years contemplating why a headmistress should never carry a gun.

What medical student became instantly infamous as the "Craigslist Killer"?

Phillip Markoff. Privileged and good looking, the 22-year old year medical student used Craigslist to troll for potential victims that he planned to rip off to pay his alleged gambling debts. The women he lured to meet him were all internet escorts and/or offered some sort of exotic service on the site that may have contributed to the perception of them being easy marks.

Rape was said not to be part of Markoff's modus operandi but beating and robbing the women he successfully ensnared was. He allegedly struck one of the victims in the head before he shot and killed her. Indicted by a grand jury for the first degree murder of Julissa Brisman in April of 2009, Markoff committed suicide shortly thereafter while in jail awaiting trial and ended his brief sociopathic 15 minutes.

What notorious diaries were declared fake but turned their forager into an instant international celebrity anyway?

Hitler's. The so-called *Hitler Diaries* were published

by West Germany's popular news magazine, *Stern*, after a slew of "experts" authenticated them prior to their purchase. Much to the embarrassment of the magazine the diaries were ultimately proven an elaborate hoax but not before their forager, Konrad Kujau, spent a lot of their money. He bought several European villas, some fancy cars, and enjoyed a few very expensive vacations before he was finally caught, tried and convicted.

After being released from prison for his part in the artful fraud, Kujau didn't let his talents go to waste. He set up shop and continued to profit off his 15 minutes selling "original Kujau forgeries." Apparently, there's some kind of loophole that legitimizes forgery if such activities are declared up front.

What heiress to a storied fortune got her 15 minutes as a bank robber and urban guerilla?

Patricia Hearst aka "Tania." 19-year-old Hearst was kidnapped at gunpoint from her apartment in the Oakland, California, in 1974 by members of the SLA, Symbionese Liberation Army, an urban guerilla group that said it wanted to liberate the planet from corporate subjugation and exploitation. The SLA had Hearst demand millions of dollars in ransom from her wealthy family (her grandfather was Randolph Hearst who built the famous Hearst Castle in California). The money was then used to buy food which was distributed to needy people in the Bay area.

After the ransom was paid the group refused to release Hearst. According to law enforcement and the media, the teenager eventually became a "willing" member of the SLA. Whatever the case, she was famously captured on camera as she robbed a San Francisco bank on April 15, 1974, wielding a machine gun and barking orders. At the time an iconic photo of Tania wearing a Che Guevara-style beret, machine gun in hand, standing in front of the SLA's notorious seven-headed snake logo went viral in the news media.

The SLA was finally quashed in 1975 in a violent and fiery shootout at their Los Angeles hideout. "Tania" wasn't there at the time and went on to rob more banks with the remaining members of the group. When she was finally arrested after almost two years on the lam, her attorney claimed Hearst was suffering from "Stockholm Syndrome," a psychological condition characterized by the victim developing an attachment with their captor to the point of identifying and becoming sympathetic with him/her/them.

Unfortunately for Hearst, the defense didn't work and she was sentenced to prison. At the time of her trial the Stockholm Syndrome was poorly understood and not yet recognized as a psychological disorder. Her prison time, however, was fortunately commuted to two years by President Carter and President Clinton later pardoned her.

A willing participant in her notoriety or not, Hearst has since spent her life out of the limelight and off the grid with Bernard Shaw, the bodyguard she married shortly after she got out of prison.

Whose heroic actions made this man an Instant Celebrity when he safely landed his plane in the Hudson River?

Captain Chelsey Sullenberger aka "Sully." His extraordinary skill and quick thinking as a pilot of a US Airways plane saved the lives of 150+ people when he ditched his distressed craft in the Hudson River on January 15, 2009. Realizing he couldn't make it back to the airport he had just taken off from because of a bird strike, "Sully" calmly informed the air traffic controllers, "We're going to be in the Hudson."

Sullenberger got his 15 minutes after his emergency landing in the Hudson River by virtue of real ability. Most would agree - it's nice to see fame visit someone who actually deserves it.

What news executive favorite of Rupert Murdock was charged with conspiracy "to pervert the course of justice" in Britain's now infamous tabloid phone-hacking scandal in 2011?

Frizzy-redheaded, believe-me-I-don't-want-to-be-an-Instant Celebrity Rebeekah Brooks. The once powerful chief executive of Murdock's *News International* and former editor of his tabloid papers, *The News of the World* and *The Sun*, once enjoyed immense prestige hobnobbing with the rich and the famous as well as many notable politicians, including several British prime ministers.

However, after the scandal revved up, Ms. Brooks was very anxious to fade into anonymity as fast as she could when it was alleged that she had her hand in one too many felonious cookie jars. Under her media watch celebrities, royals, politicians, etc., were all said to have been routinely hacked in order to get the titillating and often shocking stories her tabloid papers published.

The hacking may have continued if not for the considerable scandal caused by the hacking of missing schoolgirl Milly Dowler's voice mail. Apparently, the girl's voice mails were being hacked and then regularly deleted while Brooks was in charge of Murdock's media interests in Britain. Sadly, the deleted voice mails gave Milly Dowler's bereft parents the continuing hope their daughter was still alive when, in fact, she had already been murdered.

The ensuing scandal resulted in the closure of *The News of the World* and in Brooks' resignation as chief executive from *News International*. The scandal rocked Murdock's media empire from top to bottom and resulted in many managed resignations and firings in a transparent effort to control the damage.

Brooks faces years in prison if convicted of all the charges, but don't count on it. Knowing everyone's secrets, as she does, she continues to have powerful and influential friends everywhere.

What reality star dispenses advice on everything from haunted nurseries to the benefits of breast milk?

Rosie Pope of *Pregnant in Heels*. Under the catchy, self-promoting mantle of Maternity Concierge, Rosie has offered and continues to offer advice on just everything – even the correct way to wrap up or swaddle your baby before feeding him or her. Her advice pantry also includes tips on how to pick the right nanny as well as sage counsel on using surveillance cameras to spy on the babysitter.

Dr. Benjamin Spock must be rolling over in his grave. Really!? Maternity Concierge!? Never mind the highfalutin handle, it has conferred Instant Celebrity status on Rosie Pope and won her enough followers to launch her West Coast Rosie Pope Maternity store. Packaging is everything in the new Warholian world of my 15 minutes of fame and Rosie not only knows how to get it, but what to do with it.

What reality show features the repossession of just about anything and everything?

Lizard Lick Towing. The show has made an Instant Celebrity out of self-admiring Ron Shirley, the owner of a repo business by the same name. Whether it be the recovery of vehicles, a swamp fan boat, a herd of whitetail deer, or whatever, this series has it all including a lot of crazy, hyped-up behavior. Of course, there's a book - *Lizard Tales*, in which author Ron shares his clever, and sometimes not-so clever, turns of phrase such as, "...go fart peas at the new moon."

What reality show turned a bunch of young, badly behaving, crass-talking nobodies into somebodies – at least for a moment?

Jersey Shore. Few reality shows mirror popular culture the way this show does – at least in Jersey. The show premiered in December of 2009 in Seaside Heights, New Jersey. Often spoofed as Sleazeside Heights the show's over tanned cast of players typifies what it means "to born without the shame gene." To say that the players behave badly is a gross understatement.

The cast of characters on the show will say and do almost anything – nothing seems off limits – and while much of what they prattle on about is mean-spirited, some of it is almost funny if it were not so frequently at the expense of others.

For example, a "grenade" for a Jersey Shorite means an ugly girl who hangs out with an attractive one. BGFs (best guy friend) will fall on a grenade for their buddies so they can make a play for her hot chick friend. Another piece of slang is "motorboat." If a guy goes motor boating, he is cuddling his face between large breasts.

The cast is a sideshow of improbable and sometimes amusing comments. Snooki lets you know that she has real boobs, that Paul D. has a pierced penis, that Mike "Abs" Sorrentino trademarked the acronym "GTL" – gym, tan, laundry, as if it were earthshakingly important. Jennifer, or "JWOWW," stated unabashedly that "after I have sex with a guy, I will rip their heads off." Charming, isn't she? It conjures up the image of a preying mantis – the insect that gnaws off her partner's head after mating with him.

One burns to tell this bunch to get over themselves but it would undoubtedly be a waste of breath. As long as fans continue to feed the cast's narcissistic notions of self-importance, the *Jersey Shore* players will go on basking in the limelight of Instant Celebrity without ever realizing they're actually famous for absolutely nothing except their big mouths and rude behavior.

News Flash! MTV announced that *Jersey Shore* will start its sixth and final season in October, 2012. All you fist pumpers out there will no doubt lament its exit into impending oblivion.

What popular reality show features sisters whose most prominent physical assets are their colossal behinds?

Keeping Up with the Kardashians. Much like the *hormiga culona*, the big-butted ant of Colombia, the sisters' gargantuan derrieres cannot be missed and are self-admittedly - by them - one of most their prized assets (no pun intended).

The Kardashians would be remiss if they did not use their Instant Celebrity status to brand a line of *hormiga culona* products featuring their likeness along side one of the big-butted ants since the tasty little species is rapidly becoming a rising star in its own right - as a popular delicacy.

The reigning queen of the Kardashian clan is Kim, a publicity hound with a real nose for the big story. Her much touted and carefully managed "fairytale" marriage to jock, Kris Humphries, no doubt made her a bundle off the publicity it generated. Never mind that their nuptials ended a mere 72 days later.

Many reasons are given for the split, one as inscrutable as the other. It is rumored Kim's friends thought Mr. Humphries was a fame seeker who used Kim to fulfill his marquee dreams. Really! Krafty Kris out-maneuvered Kim at her own game!? Devastated by the break up, Kim busied herself with ever more self-promotion.

What mean-spirited behavior targeting school bus monitor, Karen Klein, turned her into an Instant Celebrity?

Bullying. After a cell video was posted on Facebook and YouTube showing middle school kids hurling abusive epithets at her and making fun of her weight, Karen became one of the most popular abuse victims ever. One million viewers saw how she was treated and rallied to her defense. As a result, the kids were forced to apologize to her and the kicker, an online fund was started for the 68-year old which has topped well over a half a million dollars affording Karen a nice retirement fund. Now she will never have to worry about smart-mouthed youngsters again. In a nice move she used $100,000 of the money to start the Karen Klein Anti-Bullying Foundation.

How is "Auto Tune," a techie invention of the Gregory Brothers, making Instant Celebrities out of so many unsuspecting people?

It uses their speeches, rants, utterances, etc., and converts them into songs. Auto Tune does this by transforming the syllables of the spoken word into musical notes. The Gregory Brothers then splits their profits with those whose verbalizations they "songify."

Such was the case of Antoine Dobson whose impassioned interview on the local TV news in Huntsville, Alabama, in 2010 about the attempted rape of his sister, Kelly Dobson, was "songified" by the Gregory Brothers and turned into the "Bed Intruder Song." The song made Antoine not only an Instant Celebrity but a bundle of change as well. The "Bed Intruder Song" sold over half a million copies at $1.30 a pop.

The same musical metamorphosis was applied to Charlie Sheen's now famous "Winning" rant and also to Christine O'Donnell's "I Am not A Witch" apologia during her 2012 presidential primary bid.

Of course, there is a phone app for those who want to turn their words into song. iPhone has a version of it and so does Droid.

What reality show has divided like an out-of-control amoeba and spawned multiple spin-offs?

Keeping Up with the Kardashians. The spin-offs include *Kourtney and Khloe Take Miami, Kourtney and Kim Take New York* and *Khloe and Lamar.* There will no doubt be others as the amoebic Kardashian brand does everything it can to keep proliferating and ensure they keep their 15 minutes going.

Note: The Palins, Osbournes and Gosselins also have or have had multiple reality shows on the air.

How do Instant Celebrities make money on "Dial A Star"?

They charge. The service offers fans a way to call

and chat up some of their favorite stars for a price - not A-Listers, of course, just run-of-the-mill reality stars, television personalities, and sundry other wannabes of the minute.

At one time you could reach Tila Tequila, Octomon Nayda Suleman, and even Dina Lohan, Lindsey's mom, for their going rate, whatever that was. In her Instant Celebrity heyday Rachel Uchitel, one of Tiger Woods' alleged dalliances, was supposedly reachable for $20 a minute.

Which kind of prime time shows get their 15 minutes peddling details about the "latest" shocking, and often gruesome, news stories?

Crime shows. The prime time ghouls headlining these shows feast on the worst in human nature to go after ratings and it works. Abductions and grisly murders top the list of the sensational crimes they go on about ad nauseam.

After all, how often is it actually edifying to speculate about the crimes of Casey Anthony one day to the next, one week to the next, even one month to the next, while other egregious misdeeds go unmentioned. Maybe it's because other crimes aren't titillating, or "sexy," enough to be covered on television. It seems that pretty, young mothers from dysfunctional families with alleged murderous instincts grab the highest ratings, as do good-looking and/or rich victims.

No matter what these primetime Instant Celebrity

ghouls may call themselves, or how much they rationalize their unsavory contribution to the noisy American psyche, their shows rarely educate the viewer in any meaningful way. Perhaps it is the insanity that believes the lie that makes them think they do. "Murder as entertainment" (could not source who originally said this) is never healthy, only desensitizing.

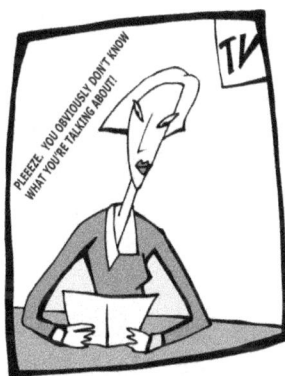

What documentary television series featured an Elvis impersonator with a serious mental issue?

Hoarding: Buried Alive. Cary Elvis's obsession with hoarding may endanger his Instant Celebrity status imitating The King - at the very least. The show makes clear how serious the compulsion is and how destructive it is to the hoarder's well being, endangering not only their social relationships and careers, but everything about their lives.

Hoarding: Buried Alive is one show that offers professional help to its participants by way of therapists and de-cluttering experts. Hoarding is a serious mental disorder and successful rehabilitation can be very difficult.

What good-looking geek literally became famous overnight following the Mars Curiosity landing in August of 2012?

Bobak Ferdowsi. When the young, enthusiastic scientist was spotted on NASA TV after Mars Curiosity's historic landing, his Tweeter followers jumped from some 200 to almost 40,000 in 24 hours according to one internet source.

Celebrated on social media as the "Nasa Mohawk Guy" because of his reddish mohawk haircut and a star inked on the shaved part of his head, the NASA JPL systems engineer was stunned at his sudden popularity. After the success of the Mars Curiosity Mission, Bobak said he realized "there were internet things going on" but was at a loss to understand all the fuss being made about him and why he was trending on social media.

This nerd's good looks and big winning smile are bringing the space program a lot of needed notice from unexpected quarters. Trying to deflect attention away from himself, Bobak said that "People should be excited about the science of this mission... I'm hoping people will follow along for at least a few months when we get all of this crazy science, and I think people will be shocked."

Bobak's Instant Celebrity will undoubtedly drive his many followers to the NASA website for more glimpses at the space program's new rock star. If smart, NASA will capitalize on his current viral popularity.

What profession has jumped on the Instant Celebrity bandwagon to hawk advice?

Doctors and some of them have become very famous. Any number of TV shows feature doctors in various specialties intent on grabbing their 15 minutes. Much of their information is good and helpful, but in the interest of filling up their programming time slot, they sometimes dispense a one-size-fits all kind of advice.

Without all the proper caveats, which is very near impossible considering the magnitude of their viewing audiences, the Hippocratic Oath they took when becoming a doctor - "To Do No Harm" - is difficult to practice in any meaningful way on television.

What television series features celebrities going bump in the night with the paranormal?

Celebrity Ghost Stories. Phantoms make for very good ratings especially when Hollywood celebs happen to spot them. Even if the ghostly stories featured on the series are not true, tweets one viewer, they still make for interesting viewing. That might be the rub.

Many of the personalities appearing on the show are not exactly A-Listers anyway so the series gives all the sort-of-famous people and/or wannabes a big opportunity to extend their run at fame for another 15 minutes or attempt to seize their first 15, whichever the case may be.

How did 12-year old Nathan Sorrell come by his 15 minutes during the 2012 London Olympic Games?

He starred in Nike's "Find Your Greatness" Olympic ad. In it the 5'3" 200 pound Nathan was shown jogging, lumbering might be a better description for it, on a lonely, country road. Social media and the internet were soon abuzz with comments about the young man, both critical and supportive. Some quarters even expressed cynicism about why Nathan had been picked to star in the ad in the first place. Was it exploitation? Contrasted with the fit specimens in the London Olympics the choice of such an overweight boy to represent Nike seemed odd at best.

Other observations were kinder and took a different tack. They said the Nike ad could be interpreted as motivational. Perhaps other kids would leave their computers, TVs, video games, iPads, etc., and go for a jog. Whatever, billions saw Nathan's Nike ad during the Olympics and it garnered him untold publicity and made him into an Instant Celebrity, albeit an uneasy one and probably not for long.

In an appearance with Matt Lauer on the *Today Show* in August of 2012, the youngster said his ad had brought out a lot of "haters" but there were also a lot of supporters out there. He hoped he would be an inspiration for them.

Who is six-year old Honey Boo Boo and what made her such a big Instant Celebrity?

Alana Thompson aka Honey Boo Boo is a child beauty pageant contestant who appeared in *Tots and Tiaras* and now has her own reality show on TLC. *Here Comes Honey Boo Boo* features the pint-sized tot from Georgia along with her redneck family.

Honey Boo Boo's winning and/or obnoxious ways, depending on your point of view, never fail to amaze and flabbergast. In fact, the whole Thompson family is a mind-bending adventure in a sideshow looking glass. Half the time you can't believe what you're seeing or hearing but you keep on looking and listening anyway.

In the first episode of *Here Comes Honey Boo Boo* Alana and the whole Thompson family go to the Redneck Games. There several members take part in the "Mudpit Belly Flop" while one daughter bobs for pig's feet. June, the mother of the clan, says the games are sort of the redneck version of the Olympics "with a lot of butt crack showing and missing teeth" – that it's all about southern pride. Wrap your mind around that one.

Honey Boo Boo is a real ham whether on the pageant stage or mugging for her reality show. Her gift for gab launches many notable one-liners like "a dolla makes me holla." Yep, right to the bank. In fact, other than her reality show this hobbit-sized Instant Celebrity has even marketed her own ringtones including "Hello! Anybody There? "Honey Boo Boo Waits on Nobody," "Dolla Makes Me Holla," and "Ring! Ring! It's Honey Boo Boo."

Honey Boo Boo has an ego far beyond her size boasting that if she practices her pageant strut and stuff enough, she could one day be Miss America. Who knows? In today's new normal anything is possible even a kid with a motor mouth and a tea-cup pig called Glitz*.

* Glitz is a consolation prize given to Alana by the rest of the Thompson family after she lost a beauty contest. Poor pig. You can tell little porky does not want to be a reality TV star.

The Instant Celebrity

Who won $50,000 in a 2012 national texting contest and extended his 15 minutes as America's fastest texter for a second straight year?

Austin Wierschke. Austin had to text forwards, backwards, and blindfolded faster than any other contestant to win the title for a second year in a row and get the $50,000 prize money. The newly minted Instant Celebrity says he plans to use the funds for college. In the meantime he is enjoying the fame spotlight giving interviews and appearing on TV shows.

FYI: Austin employs few abbreviations when texting and prefers to use correct grammar. The champ said he sends around 10,000 texts a month. Obviously, the fastest digits in the west will soon have someone come thumbing for him.

Whose screechingly awful voice on *American Idol* not only got him 15 minutes, but a record deal as well?

William Hung's. His pathetic rendition of "She Bangs" (a Ricky Martin hit) on *American Idol*'s third season and his pitiful imitation of Martin's sexy moves didn't get Hung invited back for the next round of the show. In fact, following his performance Simon Cowell shellacked him, "You can't sing, you can't dance, what do you want me to say?" Unchastened and undeterred, Hung's responded, "I already gave my best, and I have no regrets at all." Subtext: So take that, Cowell!

Hung's positive attitude, total obliviousness to his lack of talent, and quick counter to Cowell's withering criticism of his performance sparked an immediate cult following. Fan websites popped up like mushrooms all over on the web and reportedly got him over four million hits the first week alone.

Hung was invited on a slew of television shows, featured in magazines, lampooned on *Saturday Night Live* and the kicker, he inked a record deal with Koch Entertainment. He was reportedly given a $25,000 advance for making three albums that featured him singing rock and pop songs.

What hurdler turned her time in the Olympic spotlight into gold, but not the medal kind?

Attractive, media-savvy Lolo Jones. Though she did not place in her sport, she managed the media so well you would have thought she had won more gold than Michael Phelps. In HBO's *Real Sports* Lolo got up front and inappropriately personal, it would seem to some, saying she had not found the right guy yet and claimed she was still a virgin, adding she wanted to save herself until marriage - her virginity was to be a gift to her husband.

All this cozily coy talk came after Lolo had done a semi-nude layout for the Body Issue of *ESPN The Magazine*. As a result of this and other publicity, Lolo Jones became a very famous Olympic contender – quite remarkable in light of the fact she never won anything.

In a scathing piece that appeared in the August 8, 2012 edition of *The New York Times*, reporter Jere Longman said the media's focus on Lolo Jones was "not based on achievement but on her exotic beauty and on a sad, cynical marketing campaign. Essentially, Jones has decided to be whatever anyone wants her to be – vixen, virgin, victim – to draw attention to herself and the many products she endorses." The title of Longman's piece, "For Lolo Jones, Image is Everything," says it all.

But how can you blame Lolo Jones? She was just trying to get a preview of her 15 minutes. At least she had a shot at true greatness based on all her training, discipline and sacrifice. That is more than most 15 minuters can claim.

Who seared their way into the public consciousness when they famously streaked across the stage of the 46th Annual Academy Awards butt naked?

Robert Opel.   As veteran actor, David Niven, was about to introduce Elizabeth Taylor, the young man ran out from behind him and "streaked" across stage into his 15 minutes of rather foolish glory. On seeing the naked man the audience broke out in a twitter of nervous laughter. The unflappable Niven smiled and never missed a beat as he quipped, "Isn't it fascinating to think that probably the only laugh that man will ever get in his life is stripping and showing his shortcomings."

Note: During the 1960s and 70s "streakers" were part of pop culture. Initially, streaking was a way to express dissent and was most often done by men. As such, you never knew when someone might streak into a political or social event or, in many cases, a nationally televised sporting event and bare their wherewithal - sometimes just as a practical joke.

What prisoner abuse scandal made Lynndie England into a notorious Instant Celebrity when photos of her torturing Iraqi captives were secretly released?

Abu Graib. Iraqi prisoners held at the now infamous prison, or Baghdad Correctional Facility, were tortured, humiliated and sodomized (to mention just a few of the things done to them) in flagrant violation of the Geneva Convention.

Lynndie England and her ex-fiancée, Charles Graner, were two of the torturers, among others, charged and sentenced to prison in 2005. It isn't clear how high up the chain of command consent for torturing Abu Graib prisoners actually went. Some speculate it reached into the highest levels.

When pictures of prison abuse were smuggled out of Abu Graib, the world was introduced to Lynndie England. Even the great Inquisitor himself, Torquemada, would have had trouble besting her innovative and imaginative approach to torture. Her repertoire included physical, psychological and sexual abuse. In one picture she is seen with a cigarette dangling out her mouth cheekily hamming it up for the camera as she points to a naked Iraqi being forced to masturbate in front of her. In second photo she is seen holding a dog leash tied around another prisoner's neck, also naked, lying on the floor. While other American guards at the prison committed equally, and even more egregious offenses than Lynndie, it was the many snapshots of her cocky pus that turned her into a instant poster girl for the Abu Graib scandal.

Perhaps the most unforgettable picture taken at Abu

Graib is of a tortured man posed like a scarecrow wearing a black shroud with a pointed hood covering his head and face.

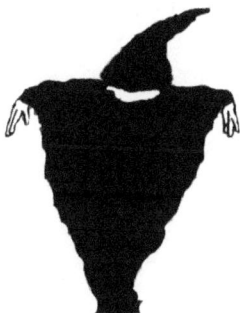

Note: The Abu Graib prison was set for demolition not long after the scandal broke.

What girls' band was convicted of "hooliganism" and sentenced to several years in jail for staging a protest against Russia's Prime Minister, Vladimir Putin?

The punk band Pussy Riot. Accused of undermining the social order for staging an anti-Kremlin, anti-Putin protest in a Moscow cathedral, charges were not initially brought against the band and may not have been if a video of their protest hadn't gone viral two weeks later.

The internet hits showing the women lambasting Prime Minister Putin turned them into international celebrities which both embarrassed and angered Russian authorities. The government soon charged the band with "hooliganism motivated by religious hatred."

Before going on trial the group was hardly heard of outside Russia. Now almost everyone has heard of them. As a result of their perceived persecution, celebrities have come to Pussy Riot's rescue, especially after the Russian court handed them down a guilty verdict in 2012.

International protests were sparked by the court's decision. Madonna spoke out on the group's behalf and she, along with others, demanded the women be freed.

Hoo   Li   Gan   =   s

What South Korean pop star's internet video has gotten 800 million+ views on YouTube?

Jae-Sang Park's aka PSY (short for Psycho). The 35-year old, chubby pop/rapper became an overnight internet sensation with his song "Gangnam Style" in the summer of 2012.

PSY's web fame launched him onto the international stage where he seems to be enjoying every second of his new found celebrity. The world has wholeheartedly embraced the goofy moves he makes in "Gangnam Style" and is now imitating them everywhere, even on *Saturday Night Live*. By the end of 2012 PSY's "Gangnam Style" had become the most downloaded video of all time.

In September, 2012, he appeared on America's *Video Music Awards*, was booked on *Ellen* and other TV shows. His Instant Celebrity status was more than validated when he was signed by Justin Bieber's manager and, just like Justin, it looks like this internet phenom might be a big new star in the making, able to turn his 15 minutes into something much longer than 15 minutes.

Note: According to PSY, Gangnam refers to a neighborhood in Seoul, not unlike Beverly Hills, which "Gangnam Style" satirizes.

Who was conferred Instant Celebrity status just because of who her sister is?

Pippa Middleton, the sister of Kate Middleton, who married Prince William. She was quoted in *The Daily Mail* as saying, "It's bit startling to achieve global recognition…on account of your sister, your brother-in-law and your bottom."

Who is Katelynne Cox and how did she come by her 15?

By writing a song about it called "15 Minutes of Fame." Her catchy lyrics capture it well. Here is a sampling:

> You won't stop 'til you get there
> Forget who you left behind
> No need to remember
> 'Cause you won't need them now.

> All you want is 15 minutes of fame
> Sell your soul for people who know your name
> 15 minutes of fame
> Throw your heart away to play the game.

Who found their 15 minutes strumming on a ukulele and singing "Tiptoe Through the Tulips"?

Herbert Khaury aka Tiny Tim. When Tiny Tim, who is actually very tall and thin, discovered he could sing in a falsetto/vibrato voice while playing his ukulele, he found the combination of stuff that would turn him into an Instant Celebrity in the 1960s.

Khaury's unusual appearance and odd voice made him a favorite on the Johnny Carson's *Tonight Show*. In fact, one of highest ratings ever for Carson was when

The Instant Celebrity

Tiny Tim married Victoria Mae Budinger, or Miss Vicki as Tiny Tim called her, on the *Tonight Show*.

Tiny Tim's Instant Celebrity got him record deals and bookings in Vegas, at least for a while. As he enjoyed his 15 minutes, critics wondered whether or not Tiny Tim's droll mannerisms might not be an elaborate put on.

As it turned out, Tiny Tim's eccentricities were the real deal. He was every bit as odd as he seemed – a romantic, modern day *Don Quixote* who found his Dulcinea in Miss Vicki. A journalist, or someone (cannot source the quote), observed of Tiny Tim that he was "a lonely outcast intoxicated by fame."

Who writer/poet/essayist/lecturer said, "Fame is proof that people are gullible"?

Ralph Waldo Emerson. When it comes to the Instant

Celebrity, Emerson seems to have gotten it just about right.

What James Bond actor made only one film for the famous franchise and then quickly disappeared from sight?

George Lazenby. *On Her Majesty's Secret Service* was Lazenby's first and only Bond film. Before the movie was even released he said he no longer wished to play the famous spy because of the way the producers had treated him while making the film. He said, "They made me feel like I was mindless." He also said that "Bond is a brute," adding, "I've already put him behind me. I will never play him again."

Whatever the ultimate reasons behind Lazenby's bruised ego, he was never asked to reprise the Bond role and his Instant Celebrity quickly slipped away. The reviews of *On Her Majesty's Secret Service*, and his performance in the film, were mixed at best.

What judge briefly made a name for himself during the Anna Nicole Smith trial?

Larry Seidlin. He famously presided over the 2007 body custody hearing of Anna Nicole Smith in Florida. During the proceedings the judge often joked and tossed out one-liners in a seeming attempt, so say some, to get his own television show a lá *Judge Judy*. Others say no, Seidlin was/is just that way – a bit corny, a bit theatrical, a bit over the top.

Whatever the case, the judge came under withering criticism for his handling of the Anna Nicole case. His behavior was characterized by some critics as less than professional. They point out that he offered commentary when not appropriate, wept at times, and made odd jokes. If he wanted to be on the national judicial map, this trial certainly put Seidlin there, but not in the way he may have wished.

Though the "Crybaby Judge," as some referred to him, did get his 15 minutes, he never got his own television show. Histrionics are welcomed fare on reality shows, but not necessarily on legal ones.

Whose iconic one-liner, "I see ghosts," turned a child actor into an Instant Celebrity?

Joel Osment's. The kid's terrific acting in the 1999 film, *The Sixth Sense*, with Bruce Willis earned him an Academy Award nomination.

Though Osment subsequently appeared in many other films including *Secondhand Lions* and *A.I. Artificial Intelligence* to praise and awards, his breakout role as Cole Sear in *The Sixth Sense* seems to have been the beginning and end of his 15 minutes, at least for the time being.

What security guard became instantly famous, and then just as quickly notorious, during 1996 Summer Olympics?

Richard Jewell. After discovering a pipe bomb at Centennial Olympic Park in Atlanta, Georgia, Jewell notified authorities and quickly helped clear the area, no doubt saving countless lives. As a result, he was called a hero and became a huge Instant Celebrity.

In the days following his actions, however, Jewell went from hero to suspect, and became the most vilified man in America when the press reported he was the FBI's prime suspect based on their profiling of him as the "lone bomber." Though he was never charged or convicted, the suspicions cast on Jewell hurt him both personally and professionally.

When Eric Rudolph, the man actually responsible for planting the bomb was apprehended many years later, Richard Jewell's name was finally cleared. In 2006 the governor of Georgia thanked the one-time prime suspect for his heroic actions in Centennial Olympic Park and for all the lives he had most surely saved that day.

Once he was fully exonerated Richard Jewell filed lawsuits against the media outlets that libeled him and demanded they apologize. He said it wasn't about money – he just wanted his name cleared by the press that had condemned him and made his life such a nightmare for so many years.

What journalist's plagiarized and fabricated stories made him more famous when his misdoing was exposed than he ever was before?

Jayson Blair's. He was a reporter for *The New York Times* until his deceptive activities were uncovered. Not only did Blair's actions torpedo his career, they also besmirched the reputation of the newspaper.

In a seeming apologia for what he had done Jayson Blair later claimed he was bi-polar. Between the lines he seemed to be suggesting that his mood disorder might be partially responsible for the fictitious and/or derivative news stories that comprised bulk of his career.

Who killed 77 people in one day and became one of the biggest mass murderers of all time?

Anders Breivik. On July 22, 2011, the murderous rampage of this Norweigan right winger made him instantly infamous. Sentenced to prison in August, 2012, people will no longer have to think about Breivik any more than anyone has to think about Charles Manson, except when he's up for parole.

What hook-up turned Kevin Federline into an Instant Celebrity?

His marriage to Britney Spears. Though he had been a backup dancer for some top celebrities no one had really heard of him until Britney looked in his direction and decided to say, "I do," with him.

The volatile hook-up with Spears did not last long but long enough to produce two kids and two singles by hubby, "Y'all ain't Ready" and "PopoZão." Federline's subsequent debut album, *Playing with Fire*, didn't do any better than his singles, perhaps even worse. The critics savaged it.

Since his controversial marriage to and divorce from Britney Spears, Kevin Federline has once again gone the way of most all Instant Celebs – into instant obscurity.

What American soldier had her Instant Celebrity status unwillingly thrust on her by the U.S. military?

Jessica Lynch. While serving in Iraq during 2003 her convoy was ambushed. The Humvee in which she was riding came under fire and was hit by a rocket-propelled grenade. Severely injured, Lynch ended up in an Iraqi hospital.

The Pentagon initially said Lynch had fought back bravely when her convoy came under attack when, in fact, she never fired off a shot. A few weeks later the military backpedaled and denied its earlier press releases portraying her as a "Rambo from the hills of West Virginia," saying it now appeared that Lynch had been too severely injured to do battle at the time of the attack. The fog of war or, was it the Pentagon's need to create fictional heroics?

When Lynch was finally able to address what had been written about her, especially by *The Washington Post*, she made it clear she was not a heroine. "That wasn't me. I'm not about to take credit for something I didn't do...I'm just a survivor."

In the testimony that she later gave before the United States House Committee on Oversight and Government Reform Lynch said, "I am still confused as to why they chose to lie and tried to make me a legend when the real heroics of my fellow soldiers that day were, in fact, legendary." She also said, "The truth of war is not always easy to hear but it always more heroic than the hype."

What exceedingly dangerous Russian sport, now going viral, has made 20-year old student, Marat Dupri, an Instant Celebrity?

"Skywalking." Participants in this dangerous sport risk their lives hundreds of feet above the ground navigating the edges of tall buildings, dangling steel girders, and any other sky-scraping structures they can find. For obvious reasons, they are called "roofers."

Marat initially climbed around on regular rooftops with his camera in hopes of getting great shots and soon realized he would have to go much higher to get what he was after. In one shot taken by another skywalker Marat is shown with arms raised outward perched at the end of steel beam impossibly high above the ground. One's stomach does flip flops just looking at the picture (see it on the web). The view below Marat is as beautiful as it is fear producing - not a sport for acrophobics.

Marat says he is a roofer because it's a way to get incredible photographs, unlike anything anyone else he is taking, and the dizzying heights give him an adrenalin rush. In fact, most roofers will tell you they do it not only for its exhilarating thrill, but also because of what most of them seek – fame and celebrity.

What Bible-thumping preacher was propelled out anonymity onto the international stage in 2010?

Terry Jones. His intolerance and bigotry made him instantly famous - for a few days anyway - when he threatened to burn the *Koran* back in 2010 on the anniversary of 9/11. Jones promoted the occasion as "International Burn A Koran Day." The Florida preacher finally backed off his threat after a few high-profile phone calls were made to him. No one seems to know if he changed his mind himself or was persuaded by one of the callers.

In 2012 Jones got to bask in another 15 minutes of notoriety when the now infamous YouTube video, *Innocence of Muslims*, was posted online. What Jones's actual association with the video was, if any, is unclear, but he seized the opportunity to continue his anti-Islam rants and stir a pot that was already boiling over.

Before going on *Master Chef* and getting her 15 minutes, what single mom was unemployed and living in a small LA apartment?

Monti Carlo. If the name sounds made up, maybe it is. The aspiring chef was once a stand-up comic and may have wanted a catchy stage name at the time.

Ms. Carlo auditioned for *Master Chef* with her recipe for apple pie. She boxed up her sample of sweet Americana in an empty diaper container and stood in line with 1,000 other hopefuls. Why she chose this particular container is debatable. Was it a ploy to curry favor with the judges? Perhaps. Whatever, she did get invited on the show and ultimately came in fifth in the *Master Chef* cooking competition.

Monti Carlo now hosts her own radio show in Phoenix, Arizona, dispensing cooking tips for busy moms. She is also writing a cook book. She said the two months she spent on *Master Chef* gave her "a lot of confidence and a whole new life."

It goes to show you, even though she didn't win, Monti is taking full advantage of the 15 minutes the show gave her. She is using her Instant Celebrity to promote herself on the airwaves and stir up yet other profitable ventures.

The 2012 season of *Master Chef* has ended and the winner of the competition is Christine Ha. Blinded as a result of an autoimmune disease that attacked her optic nerve, Christine manages to cook up a storm anyway. She is quoted as saying, "Everyone is much more capable than they think they are."

Ha became proof certain of her philosophy when she won $250,000 in the *Master Chef* finale, got her own cookbook as a result of the win, and earned the title of *Master Chef.*

With her new celebrity status Ha plans to open restaurants and cafes. Without the credentials of the show and the cachet behind it, she admits this probably wouldn't have been possible. After all, who would bankroll a blind chef if she hadn't already proven herself as she did on *Master Chef?*

What 2012 internet phenom's catchy song went viral, spawned countless imitations of it, and turned her into an Instant Celebrity?

Carly Rae Jepsen's. Her song, "Call Me Maybe," caused a frenzy of good-natured spoofs and imitations, not only by Justin Bieber, but by U.S. soldiers as well as the Miami Dolphin cheerleaders – to mention just a few.

Jepsen's feel-good, addictive song quickly hopped from the internet to the radio and eventually climbed to the top of *Billboard* where it remained for weeks.

In what malodorous activity did a woman contestant participate on the reality series, *Extreme Couponing*, that conferred doubtful celebrity on her, for a jiffy anyway?

Dumpster diving. A woman called Krista did it in a desperate search for coupons. You might be of the mind that such an activity is extreme and you would be right but that is exactly what this show is about and what its viewers like. The contestants do almost anything to acquire as many coupons as they can – be it begging, borrowing, trading for, or in this case, diving for.

Whether scripted or not, such pathetic antics get big ratings. In Krista's case she was supposedly able to pay her medical expenses (she was pregnant at the time) with the dumpster's coupon proceeds.

As icky and cringe-producing as dumpster diving might be, surfing that trash Krista got her 15 minutes.

Hopefully, she will now be able to raise her offspring in the same anonymity from which she sprang.

What billionaire, inventor of a very popular energy drink, said he "liked toiling in obscurity"?

Manoj Bhargava. He didn't get his wish however; in fact, he is getting his 15 minutes right now, like it or not. When *Forbes Magazine* outed him in 2012 as a billionaire, America suddenly got to meet the founder and CEO of 5-Hour Energy - the very popular two-ounce drink that recently came under fire in connection with a number of deaths allegedly caused, at least in part, by the souped-up beverage.

Self-effacing Bhargava lives without the trappings of wealth or celebrity – meaning he has no fancy cars or homes. Even his offices are Spartan, revealing no evidence of his entrepreneurial success.

The billionaire who has stated he doesn't want to be

famous really seems to mean it, now perhaps more than ever in light of the government's investigation.

Who is stubbly-faced Grover Norquist and what made him simultaneously both so famous and so notorious?

He is America's number one tax protestor. Norquist has worked ceaselessly to get as many legislators as possible to sign a pledge to never again raise taxes.

It has been said that "he is the most powerful man in America besides the president." An exaggeration to be sure, but Norquist's sway over many in congress has contributed to its frequent deadlocks on new taxes. Those who signed the pledge have been hesitant to go back on it, afraid that Norquist and his minions would oppose their reelection. However, as the "Fiscal Cliff" loomed at the end of 2012, many politicos were seriously rethinking their pledge.

Whatever the case, as founder of Americans for Tax Reform, this Tea Party darling still has enough clout to influence political figures and is popular enough to get invited on lots of talk shows to discuss his agenda.

What 51-year old *Green Mile* actor extended his 15 minutes by another second or two when he married a 16-year old and gave his new bride a chance at the Instant Celebrity spotlight as well?

Doug Hutchinson. His 2011 Las Vegas marriage to Courtney Alexis Stoddard, a wannabe pop star, lifted the two out of obscurity. Initially, many in the media thought something was "fishy" about the nuptials – perhaps a big publicity stunt designed to benefit them both. The couple supposedly ignored all the chatter and made a point of letting everyone know the huge age difference between them didn't matter – "that true love can be ageless." Why is it then Courtney can't seem to remember she is married? The teenager says she just forgets. Duh!

Whether true love is ageless or not, celebrity seekers age fast in the media. Now most people would be hard pressed to recall either Hutchinson's or Stoddard's name and, unless one of them comes up with a hit movie or song fast, their Instant Celebrity star will no doubt be sucked into a big black hole never to be seen again.

Whose soaring version of "I Dreamed A Dream" on *Britain's Got Talent* back in 2009 stunned the judges so much so they were left with their mouths agape in amazement?

Susan Boyle's. Even Simon Cowl dropped his jaw, and his sneer, in awe of the petite Scottish singer's huge talent. Initially, the frumpy, chubby, middle-aged Susan Boyle was discounted by both audience and judges alike – that is, until she began singing.

After a nervous start, Boyle belted out a version of "I Dreamed A Dream" from *Les Misérables* that left everyone with goose bumps and a few teary eyes. Her rendition of the song was an immediate YouTube hit and led to guest appearances on television shows and lucrative recording deals. Boyle's exceptional talent seems to guarantee she is no flash in the fame pan.

What famous baseball player's career and celebrity ended because of a gambling problem?

Pete Rose's. His star flamed out as a result of an alleged addiction to gambling. Like Shoeless Joe Jackson before him, scandal ended his career and tarnished his name. Now he probably couldn't even make it as a celebrity in any venue, in or out of sports, such is his notoriety.

The all-time MLB player in hits as well as many other stats, Pete Rose was banned from professional baseball in 1989 because of gambling. Betting on sports is big no-no in the sacred temple of professional sports. Because of his habit even Pete Rose's three World Series and 4,000+ hits will not help him make into the Baseball Hall of Fame - at least not for the foreseeable future. Once you become a notorious ex-jock no one wants you around, much less in their club.

What did Leopold and Loeb do that turned them into celebrities of the notorious variety?

They committed the perfect crime in 1924 - or at least they thought they had. That was the year they carefully planned, then kidnapped and murdered 14-year old Bobby Franks in Illinois. The two perpetrators came from well-off families and were both highly intelligent. Leopold reportedly had an IQ in excess of 200 – off the charts.

The crime of which they were ultimately convicted took place when they were both in their late teens. At the time both Leopold and Loeb had already completed college and subscribed to the Nietzschean philosophy that some individuals were supermen and as such, they were exempt from the laws that governed ordinary men and were not to be held accountable for their actions.

Leopold and Loeb may have gotten away with the murder if not for a pair of eyeglasses with a unique hinge found near the body of Bobby Franks. Only three pairs of glasses with that hinge had been sold in the Chicago area, one of them to Nathan Leopold. It ultimately tied the pair to the homicide.

Though a ransom had been asked for by the duo, it

was never the motive behind the murder. According to Leopold and Loeb, it was "the thrill of the kill" and their desire to pull off "the perfect crime." But for that glass hinge, they almost did.

In what country are sheep featured on their very own reality show?

Senegal. Owners enter their prized sheep into this country's top-rated television show, *Khar Biig* (*This Sheep*), now in its fourth season. The sheep contestants are judged in several categories including but not limited to: size of entrant, coat quality, testicle proportion and symmetry, etc.

The lucky sheep that finally manages to win this reality show competition confers status and Instant Celebrity on its owner, along with a purse of $4,000.

What provocative young preacher has become famous online sermonizing against religion?

Jeff Bethke. The young and energetic Bethke won his online congregation rapping out sermons that shocked many with his disavowal of organized religion. He says he hates religion but loves Jesus. His views have enraged fundamentalists who claim he is a false prophet, even the Anti-Christ.

Pariah or not, after Bethke posted his "Why I Hate Religion, But Love Jesus" video on YouTube, he got millions of hits and ignited an on-going debate about the nature of Christianity and those who practice it. In one of his rap poems he pointedly asks, "But if Jesus came to your church would they actually let Him in?"

Many Christians are incensed with the young preacher's views and words. Notwithstanding their ire, Bethke is becoming so popular among many young people he is often asked for autographs when in public and his many admirers line up to have their pictures taken with him.

What couple's reality show captivated its viewing audience until it crashed and burned at the end of its fifth season?

Jon & Kate Plus 8. Even the couple's adorable brood of eight was not enough to save either the show or their marriage. Losing the show appeared to be more of a disappointment for Kate which she had once referred to as her job. The loss of her philandering husband, on the other hand, didn't seem to have bothered her much at all.

As for *Jon & Kate Plus 8*'s viewing audience – well, it has no doubt moved on to some other equally tedious reality show.

What self-righteous Bible thumper got caught with a hooker and tried like hell to bawl himself back to redemption on national television?

Jimmy Swaggart, the Pentecostal preacher popular with America's sinners, was now known to everyone as a result of his famous confession. In the 1980s his television ministry was aired to thousands of TV and radio stations each week.

Swaggart's histrionic and charismatic stage presence mimicked that of rock-n'roller Jerry Lee Lewis. Not surprising as Jerry Lee Lewis is his cousin. While his cousin had his own issues with women, Swaggart was swept up in a 1988 scandal of almost Biblical proportions, by Pentecostal standards at any rate, when his sexual proclivity for prostitutes was revealed by the press.

After one dalliance, Swaggart gave his famous "I Have Sinned" speech saying, "I have sinned against You, my Lord, and I would ask that Your Precious Blood wash and cleanse every stain until it is in the seas of God's forgiveness." This speech, however, was not the end of Swaggart's seeming penchant for transgression.

In 1991 he was pulled over by a California highway patrolman for allegedly driving on the wrong side of the road. Riding shotgun was a prostitute Swaggart had picked up along the way. When the patrolman asked what she was doing in the car with the preacher man she minced no words, "He asked me for sex. I mean, that's why he stopped. That's what I do. I'm a prostitute."

Who knows? Maybe that is also why Swaggart veered off on the wrong side of the road – Rosemary didn't waste any time getting down to work.

This time Swaggart did not apologize for his carnal lapse. Instead he told his congregation that "The Lord told me it's flat none of your business." Luckily, Swaggart's son stepped in and artfully explained to the astounded onlookers his father would be taking a leave of absence from the ministry for "a time of healing and counseling."

So it goes... Swaggart's celebrated ministry never recouped its glory days. However, his cringe-producing crying jag is still remembered by many to this day. Notoriety, it seems, has more staying power than the momentary popularity of any ilk, spiritual or otherwise. Swaggart is just one more example of a celebrity whose behavior turned their fame into infamy and torpedoed their career, or calling, however which way you want to look at it.

What woman set off a storm of media frenzy when she confessed to a homicide she did not commit and was then exonerated because she was "too fat to kill"?

Mayra Rosales, known as the "Half-Ton Killer" in a documentary aired by TLC, initially said the death of her two-year old nephew in 2008 was an accident. She had fallen on him and killed him. The district attorney in

Texas, however, didn't agree with her version of events and charged her with homicide to which the morbidly obese woman ultimately confessed.

Mayra's attorney later had the charges dismissed based on the defense that his client was "too fat to kill." At the time of her nephew's death, Mayra was said to be too heavy to get out of bed. The defendant supposedly confessed to the crime because she thought her weight was killing her and she wanted to take the rap for her sister who, in fact, was responsible for the crime. The sister had hit her son with a hairbrush in a fit of rage.

After the criminal proceedings were over, Mayra was finally rescued from her bed so she could get help she needed for her still ballooning 1,000+ poundage. Part of one wall of her house had to be removed before Mayra was liberated by ten able-bodied men and carted off to the hospital.

What man became a reluctant Instant Celebrity when he blew the whistle on big tobacco?

Jeffery Wigand. A former executive with Brown and Williamson, the explosive nature of Wigand's disclosures against big tobacco had him so concerned about his own safety, he hired a bodyguard. His whistle blowing and subsequent crusade against the tobacco industry was made into the 1999 film, *The Insider*, starring Russell Crowe.

The movie captures all the high drama, legal and personal, that Wigand went through when he decided to tell the truth about cigarettes. Among other things, he exposed how the industry had made them as addictive as possible and how statistics about their toxicity were manipulated to make them seem much less lethal than they were/are. All the years of industry fudging and fabrication about cigarettes was more than just cynical, it was monstrous.

SMOKE, SMOKE
THAT CIGARETTE!

Who said "Fame means millions of people have the wrong idea of who you are"?

Writer Erica Jong. It sounds like she got it just about right.

Who made a supersonic leap into international Instant Celebrity in October, 2012?

Felix Baumgartner. The Austrian daredevil broke the sound barrier when he plummeted to earth from 24 miles up in the stratosphere without the use of an aircraft.

Baumgartner broke several other records on October 14, 2012 as well, including: the highest altitude ever reached by a manned balloon; longest freefall descent; and, over 800 million simultaneous live stream views on YouTube.

Just before Baumgartner jumped to earth, he uttered the words, "I'm coming home." The daredevil said he meant it - no more stratospheric dives. Apparently, he does not want to risk his hard earned 15 minutes any time soon. And so it goes.

Who was quoted as saying, "I want a billion people to know my name as well as they know their own. I want to clone myself to fame"?

Jarod Kintz.   Apparently, it didn't work.   Who is Jarod Kintz anyway?

As well, who are most of the people in this book? Most likely nobody anyone much remembers anymore. Such is the fleeting nature of fame and the wannabe Instant Celebrities it courts.

The Instant Celebrity

Afterword

In the time you have spent thumbing through this book many new Instant Celebrities have grabbed their 15 minutes and are desperately attempting to hang on. The vast majority won't succeed and will quickly disappear, only to be replaced by the latest wannabes.

Whatever your like or dislike of media-driven celebrity, it is presently our culture's drug of choice - one that seems here to stay.

The Instant Celebrity

The Instant Celebrity

The Instant Celebrity

Other Invisibird Books in the "Instant Series" by Tanya Slover:

The Instant Genius: An Indispensable Handbook for Know-It-Alls
The Instant Voyeut: A Titillating Peek at Sex and Love
The Instant Politico: Memorable Scandals, Secrets and Gaffes
The Instant Idiot: Dumbest Things People, Famous or Not, Have Said or Done

  * Forthcoming

Invisibird Books for Children:

The Adventures of Billy the Cat

Tanya Slover is an author, poet and screenwriter.

Invisibird
Books

www.ingramcontent.com/pod-product-compliance
Lightning Source LLC
Chambersburg PA
CBHW022115280326
41933CB00007B/405